GOD

AND

WAR

Fulton J. Sheen

Title: God and War, Fulton J. Sheen, author;
edited by Allan J. Smith.

Description: Midland, Ontario: Bishop Sheen
Today, 2023.

Includes bibliographical references.

Identifiers:
ISBN: 978-1-990427-06-0 (paperback)
ISBN: 978-1-990427-93-0 (hardcover)
ISBN: 978-1-990427-07-7 (e-book)

Subjects: God – Faith – War – Prayer - Victory

To Mary

**Immaculate Mother of God,
Gracious Queen of Christ's afflicted
ones, in prayerful petition
that the Glorious Peace of Christ
may reign in the souls of men.**

CONTENTS

INTRODUCTION

When looking back on the life of
Archbishop Fulton J. Sheen, there are some
that would refer to him as 'a man for all
seasons'. Over his lifetime, he spent himself
for souls, transforming lives with the clear
teaching of the truths of Christ and His
Church through his books, radio addresses,
lectures, television series, and many
newspaper columns.

Fulton J. Sheen was born in 1895 in El
Paso, Illinois. He lived and studied through a
time in history in which he witnessed the
effects of two world wars and many social,
political, and economic conflicts.

While a graduate student and university
professor in the United States and Europe,
Sheen made friends with a number of the
great thinkers and writers of his day such as
G.K. Chesterton, Christopher Dawson, J.R.R.
Tolkien, and C.S. Lewis.

After his ordination to the priesthood in
1919, Sheen would go on to receive numerous
degrees from the Catholic University of

America, Louvain University in Belgium, and the Angelicum University in Rome.

From 1926-1950 he was a full-time professor at the Catholic University of America, first in the School of Theology and later in the School of Philosophy. At the beginning of his teaching career, Sheen was regarded with esteem as one of the premier scholars of his time. The publication of his first book in 1925, *God and Intelligence in Modern Philosophy: A Critical Study in the Light of the Philosophy of Saint Thomas*, garnered Sheen extraordinary respect for his scholarship on St. Thomas Aquinas. The book was so well received that Sheen was awarded the Cardinal Mercier International Philosophy Award. Also impressed with the content was G.K. Chesterton, whose admiration is evidenced by his willingness to write the book's introduction.

During his time at the Catholic University of America, Sheen wrote thirty-four books on various topics. He also was the featured speaker on the Catholic Hour radio broadcast, having millions of listeners tuning in each week.

Witnessing the threat of Communism on the rise in the 1920s, it became sufficiently clear to Sheen that modern atheism was not only an esoteric philosophy preached by learned professors at Harvard and Yale, but it was a new type of Messianism emanating from Moscow, threatening to cover the face of the earth. So in the same year in which Pope Pius XI issued his encyclical on atheistic Communism (1937), Fulton J. Sheen published three books titled: *'Communism', 'Communism and Religion',* and *'Liberty Under Communism'.*

Sheen stressed the need for the use of reason in dealing with Communism. On the subject matter, he was no intellectual featherweight, and he brought his formidable powers of intellect to bear on the problem of Communism, the better to refute it. He absorbed Marx, Lenin, and Stalin to prepare himself for the assaults he would sustain in his deconstruction of their theories. He was a tremendous success. He converted or influenced several Communists and leftists in the heyday of American Communism, including Louis Budenz, Elizabeth T. Bently, Bella Dodd, and Heywood Broun.

Toward the end of the 1930s, talk of war began to surface. When German forces invaded Poland on September 1, 1939, World War II began. Almost immediately Fulton J. Sheen rose to the occasion of being called to bring sense to a nation that was looking for answers to the questions of war. During his presentations on the radio he encouraged his audience to think of the great spiritual transformation that there would be in America if every Jew, Protestant, and Catholic according to the light of his conscience prayed one continuous hour a day, for the president, for Congress, and for victory.

Archbishop Sheen called World War II not only a political struggle, but also a 'theological one'. He referred to Hitler as an example of the "Anti-Christ." Sheen also said that, "the means of life no longer ministers to peace and order because we have perverted and forgotten the true ends of life... It is not our politics that has soured, nor our economics that have rusted; it is our hearts. We live and act as if God had never made us."

In 1941, the United States officially entered World War II. That same year Sheen penned the book *"A Declaration of Dependence."* In it, Sheen writes, "The Declaration of Independence, I repeat, is a Declaration of Dependence! We are independent of dictators because we are dependent on God. God is the necessary factor of our salvation. As a result, he is to be the center of our lives. His ways ought to permeate every aspect and area of our lives: education, employment, pleasure, mourning, socializing, etc. All is done in sight of the omnipotent Lord, and all we do should be done reflecting this knowledge. Our every interaction should be filled with the love of our Savior."

Numerous articles, radio reflections, and books would continue to be produced by Sheen throughout the war. Given their importance and the impact they had on society in his day, it seemed appropriate to re-release some of Archbishop Sheen's reflections on war taken from his book *God and War* (New York: P.J. Kenedy and Sons, 1942)

This book contains a collection of Sheen's Catholic Hour radio addresses that were heard by millions of listeners each week. These reflections are a series of short essays that addressed the many concerns of the listeners of his day during the war.

Sheen answers questions about the things of God in war time, trusting in God's plan, prayer in war, and the Divine path to victory. His were some of the most clearly delineated investigations into the underlying causes of the war combined with an entirely sound and hopeful program for winning both the war and the even more important peace are found in them. These powerful reflections can be most heartily recommended for their wise counsel, sane and penetrating analysis, and logical conclusions.

Sheen addresses the vexation felt by a great mass of people who were frankly dissatisfied with the ephemeral and superficial commentaries about the war. Like a master surgeon, Sheen applied the sharp scalpel of his crystal-clear logic to lay open the sources of the world's infection.

Sheen writes, "There are two ways of looking at the war: one as a journalist, the other as a theologian. The journalist tells you what happens; the theologian not only why it happens, but also what matters. Our approach is from the divine point of view, first of all, because it is the only explanation which fits the facts; secondly, because the American people who have been confused by catchwords and slogans are seeking an inspiration for a total surrender of their great potentialities for sacrifice, both for God and country."

Sheen is firm in his conviction that real peace cannot be declared, it must be made. It is with peace-making and the fundamental conditions on which peace must be based that this book is concerned. In its seven forceful and readable chapters, it challenges the theory of many planners today who posture that military allies are necessarily political allies; it affirms that a common hatred can make nations allies, but only a common love can make them neighbors; it denies the primacy of action over reason, in the sense that the will of the state is that which makes a state right; and it contends that utility does not establish justice, but it is justice which makes utility.

With the same lucid and persuasive reasoning that has made him outstanding both as a writer and as a lecturer, Sheen continues to challenge people of goodwill to unite for the preservation of personal rights, freedom of conscience, human justice, and civilization itself – all of which are in danger in the present conflict. Here, one will recognize the urgency of Sheen's subject matter, and will find pillars of peace and promise in his far-sighted principles.

Archbishop Fulton J. Sheen's destiny was encrypted in his name, for in the Gaelic language *Fulton* means *war* and *Sheen* means *peace*. Sheen's lifelong goal was to establish peace, but in that call, he inevitably came up against many obstacles toward that noble ideal. It is as though his very name foretold the kind of life he was to have: an uninterrupted warring against the powers of darkness to promote the peace of Christ's kingdom.

THE THINGS OF
GOD IN WAR TIME

In the face of the accumulating disasters in the world today the flight of refugees, the bombing of open cities, the suffering of the innocent, the spectacle of humanity preying upon itself — the modem mind asks the question: Why does God permit this war? The repeated onslaught against goodness and justice are a scandal to men; they cannot understand why God allows these things.

This question is more often asked by unbelievers than by believers. Those who know God, love Him and trust Him, are less apt to be troubled by evil, war and a cross, than those whose thinking and loving is geared to the world.

Our Divine Lord told Peter that much when after saying that He must go up to Jerusalem and be put to death and on the third day rise again, Peter took the Savior aside and rebuked Him with some anger: "Far be it from Thee, O Lord; this will never happen to Thee." (Matt 16:22)

Peter started with exactly the same assumption some do when they consider either war or suffering in relation to God; Peter assumed the Cross was a total loss, incompatible with Divine Power, and disruptive of God's purposes.

But Our Lord, turning His back on Peter, said to him whom a moment before He had called the Rock: "Get behind me, Satan, thou art a scandal to me; for thou dost not mind the things of God, but those of men." (Matt 16: 23)

Notice Our Divine Lord set in contrast "things of God" and "things of men." The "things of God" imply a cross as a prelude to glory. The "things of men" on the contrary, seek to avoid the cross, to escape the law of sacrifice, or, in the language of the modern psychologists, they seek to be "self-expressive" — which in less euphemistic language means "selfishness." That to Our Divine Lord is "scandalous."

In approaching therefore the problem of disaster in any form, there are only two possible points of view: Peter's view, that the Cross is a loss, and the Savior's view, that the Cross leads to salvation.

All who take Peter's point of view look only to the present, which is necessarily self-centered. Many there are who take that point of view today.

All who take the Savior's point of view, however, look not only to the present, but to the past and the future; to the past, because the burden of the world's sin goes to make up our present woe, to the future because by cooperating with God's purposes through sacrifice and prayer we can redeem ourselves from present and momentary defeat and by a cross enter into the blazing triumph of a New Easter and a better world.

When Our Lord made the distinction between those who "mind the things of God" and those who "mind the things of Men" he implied that it would be the unbelievers rather than the believers in God who would be troubled by a Cross, either in the form of a crucifixion, or a persecution and a war.

This is contrary to our modern way of thinking. Today the unbelievers think that the war creates an insoluble difficulty for believers. Our Lord implied just the contrary.

Who is right. Our Lord or the modern mind? Let us try to understand each. The modern mind says that war and evil make God unintelligible. To some extent they are right, for the Christian starts with the simple proposition that God is Justice and love.

But once these affirmations are made, the problem of evil is intensified, for if God is just, why is there injustice; if God is love, why is there hate and war? These are legitimate questions and they do throw a difficulty on one who "minds the things of God."

The unbeliever, the materialist, the sceptic, the sophomore who still feeds on the husks of Darwin, Marx, and James, never has to answer these questions; for if the world is only a machine, why should it not occasionally get out of order? If there is no purpose in living, then why should life not be meaningless? If we are descended from beasts why not act like beasts?

Since there is no goodness at the root of the universe, no Sun of Justice from which the rays of human rights descend, then there is no reason why these dark and awful cataclysms should not happen.

Given no Providence, why should life not be a mockery, and pessimism our lot? The existence of evil is therefore no mystery to the unbeliever, it is a "natural."

But despite all this, Our Lord still suggests that the unbeliever has the greater problem, and He is right. For although the materialist does escape the problem of evil, he runs into an insuperable difficulty which does not exist for the one who "minds the things of God," namely the problem of good.

It is not easy for us to explain why God permits evil, but it is impossible for the unbeliever to explain why good exists; he cannot tell us why a material, soul-less, God-less, crossless universe should be the center of self-sacrifice, purity, love, faith, a Cross, martyrdom, and a willingness to die rather than offend God.

John Galsworthy expressed this idea in his Maid in Waiting. The girl, Dinny, is talking to her mother, Lady Cherwell:

"I suppose there is an eternal plan," she says, "but we are like gnats for all the care it has for us as individuals."

"Don't encourage such feelings, Dinny," says her mother, they affect one's character."

"I don't see," replies the daughter, "the connection between beliefs and character. I'm not going to behave any worse because I cease to believe in Providence or an after life."

"Surely Dinny?"

"No, I'm going to behave better; if I'm decent, its because decency is the decent thing; and not because I'm going to get anything by it."

Whereupon the mother asks: "but why is decency the decent thing, Dinny, if there's no God?"

That is the ultimate problem. Why out of an unspiritual universe should spiritual lives emerge? If there is no Beauty behind the universe, whence the Rose; if there is no Justice behind the universe, then whence comes our war for justice; if there is no distinction between good and evil, then how can our enemies be evil?

The unbeliever is confronted with more baffling difficulties by a war than the believer, for he cannot explain why all those things which should have brought happiness, brought disaster.

If he asks "Where is your God now?" the believer may retort: "Where are your gods now? Where is your god Progress in the face of two world wars within 21 years? Where is your god Science, now that it consecrates its energies to destruction? Where is your god

Evolution now that the world is turned backward into one vast slaughterhouse?"

The man of faith can explain this chaos. He knows that science, art, religion, politics, economics divorced from God their final end, turn against us and destroy us, just as if we diverted gasoline from its rational purpose and used it as a beverage, it would end in our destruction.

In the language of Scripture: "Where are their gods, in whom they trusted ... let them arise and help you." (Deut. 32:37, 38)

Furthermore, the unbeliever cannot explain the growth of evil in the world. The believer can. On what does evil feed? It feeds only on the good. Evil has no capital of its own. It feeds on the capital of God. How could the Militant Atheism of Communism exist if there were no God? How could the swastika exist if there were no Cross? How could scepticism exist if there were no faith? How could Fascism exist if there were no human rights to deny? On what does persecution thrive except on faith?

You can explain evil only by the absence of good, as you can explain darkness only as the absence of light.

And that is why the unbeliever, in time of crisis and war, mouths slogans and busies himself about many things, but never settles down to the one supreme business of war: To overcome evil by good, and to drive out the devils by the finger of God.

Because I believe in God I can understand why there should be a war. Since God is love, should He not make man in such a way that by want of love pain should arise, just as through want of sun the flower should die? Evil is but a lack of love, and can be conquered only by love.

As the sun's rays pierce the cold not to warm the cold — for the cold is but the negation of heat — but to cause the sluggish air to vibrate, so can love thrill the stagnant evil with its vital force of sacrifice unto new love.

Because I believe in Christ the Son of God, I can better understand war, for why should not men hate God now, as they did when they nailed Him to a tree?

Why should not the Divine Savior who once in His human nature chose Good Friday, choose it now again in all those who are incorporated under His Headship?

True, He can never suffer again in the human nature He took from Mary, and which is now at the right hand of the Father; but He can suffer again in other human natures, in His Mystical Body, which is the Church.

Cannot He, who once set His face to Jerusalem, now set it toward Berlin, or Moscow, or Warsaw, or anywhere where Truth is crucified? Do not the Cross and the Passion need to be actualized in each new age?

Is Calvary only an historical event which happened once and will never happen again; or is it a law, which operates whenever evil becomes concentrated in persecution and injustice, that goodness might sacrifice itself as a true soldier, in order that the world perish not?

If He, who valued life more than anyone ever valued life — for He was the source of life — did not think death too great a price to pay to defeat evil, shall there not be those in each generation who, through climbing the same Golgotha, will surrender their lives in Him that the evil of their day that makes war, may be conquered again.

He made us "other Christs;" we believe that, as Christians. Then why shall not His Passion be a single unbroken act in which each of us, through our Cross, prove our right to Christhood!

The war, then, need not be for us a reason for denying God, anymore than the Cross was a reason for Peter denying Christ.

If the Cross was to a Savior a proof that there was something wrong in man that had to be righted by His sacrificial death, why should not the war be to us a proof that there is something wrong in the world that can be righted only by our sacrificial lives?

Shall we blame God when we give ourselves a headache by violating His physical law by over-drinking? Shall we blame Him when the world generates a war out of its bosom by the violation of His moral law?

Very frankly it means nothing to say that Fascism, Nazism, and Communism, Capitalism, Racism, and Militarism, caused this war. These things do not exist except in persons, and they exist only in persons who sin.

If therefore it was sin that gave Christ His Cross and sin that gave us the war, should we not take a more humble attitude, and strike our breasts to the extent that we are guilty, saying "Mea culpa" — "Through my fault"?

Should we not see ourselves as bearing part of the burden of the world's sin, and through penance and the Cross begin the world's redemption?

We are not going to win the war by calling our enemies "devils", for Our Divine Lord warned us not to rejoice that the devils were subject to us, but that our names were written in the Kingdom of Heaven. (Luke 10:20).

How shall this be done except by a rededication of ourselves to God, not as individuals but as a mass, a people, a nation?

After this war we want something we did not get in the last war.

We want not victory alone—we had that in 1918; we want not merely the defeat of Germany and its Feuhrer — we had that in 1918; we want not a revengeful treaty of peace — we had that in 1918; we want not merely to make the world safe for democracy — we had that in 1918; we want not simply the crushing of barbarism — we had that in 1918.

This time we want something that was left out of Victory, left out of Versailles; left out of the so called peace, namely, the restoration to the world of a Justice based on the morality of God.

And how shall we get it back? Only by those of us who believe in God, in prayer, in sacrifice, in the Cross and the Commandments, creating a public opinion so strong that politicians, economists, generals, and diplomats cannot ignore it.

It gets down to something as simple as this: There can be only one guarantee that the peace following this war will be different, and that is to ground it on God's moral order.

We must influence the world, and the only effective way to do it is to "mind the things of God."

It will do no good to make your demands for moral regeneration felt by wiring your congressmen, nor by holding parades, nor by signing petitions.

We must do it in the way of the French convict, whose innocence was discovered after his death and 23 years of penal servitude, and on whose tomb was inscribed: "He has gone to find Justice with God." Justice with God, nowhere else.

If we could present to the United States the spectacle of ten or fifteen million Catholics daily uniting their sacrifice for country with the sacrifice of Our Savior on the Cross,

America would begin to say of us: "They have gone to seek Justice with God."

That is our plan! If enough do it to create a mass opinion, we shall have victory and peace with justice; if not, we shall have another war.

SPECTATORS AND ACTORS IN THE DRAMA OF THE CROSS

Why does God permit this war? In this chapter we penetrate a little deeper into the mystery by showing that this question is generally asked by the spectators, not by the actors, in the drama of suffering.

It is the sufferers who manifest the greatest faith; it is the spectators who are the sceptics. No one knows this better than a priest. As we go about administering the consolation of the sacraments which Our Divine Lord provided for the suffering and the dying, we are but rarely asked: "Why does God do this to me?"

On the contrary, we find most often a positively joyful submission to the divine will, the sufferers saying: "Whatever the good Lord sends me I accept"; or "Well this suffering gives me an opportunity to do penance for my sins"; or "This will shorten my Purgatory"; or "What I suffer is nothing compared to what Jesus suffered on the Cross for me."

But as we priests leave the beds of the faithful who bear the marks of the Cross on their bodies, and go out among those whose lives are comfortable, and who never pray, who are cross because the morning paper has not arrived for breakfast, and who think that an A.B. degree gave them a mind greater than the Almighty — there we are asked: "Why does God allow war and suffering and evil?"

It is generally those who have never had a struggle in life, who never disciplined themselves, who bombard heaven with their petulant accusations and shout to God their resentful: Why? Why? Why?

On the stage of Calvary a great Actor enacted a role in the world's greatest tragedy, and after bearing the brunt of the world's evil, pronounced with strong voice and clear mind the great last line: "Father, into thy hands I commend my spirit" (Luke 23:46).

But beneath that stage, the spectators queried: "He trusted in God; let him deliver him now, if he wants him" (Matt. 27:43).

Why is it that the actors in the drama of tragedy are less puzzled by its cross than the spectators? Three reasons come to mind: Because suffering reveals love; because it initiates us into the mystery of life; and because it destroys false values.

An actor in the drama of suffering is better able to understand love than a spectator. What passes for love today is frequently nothing but selfishness. Moderns think of love in terms of having, owning, and possessing, for the pleasure it will give them.

That is not love — that is sin; that is "sex"; that is selfishness.

One of the reasons so many marriages are shipwrecked today is because the parties, thinking of love in terms of the pleasure each receives, feel that if the other no longer gives pleasure, therefore there is no love. As a result there develops in each a loathing for the other, as if the other cheated in not giving all that was desired.

Love of this kind is in the animal part of us, not in the will where love really resides, It is love without responsibility; and love without responsibility is selfishness and hate.

The truth is that we could never understand love if sacrifice were impossible. Because love means not to have but to be had, not to own but to be owned, not to possess but to be possessed, it implies sacrifice, surrender, and otherness.

All love is an act of choice: We choose this thing in preference to that, or this person in preference to that person.

Love is not just an affirmation, but a negation; it implies sacrifice — a surrender of our will, of our selfish interests, for the good of the other. It looks not to the lover's pleasure, but to the happiness of the beloved.

Love is wicked self-centeredness if there is no willingness to make a sacrifice for the one loved.

Our highest joys in life consist in feeling that another's good is purchased by us, and that our labor and our pain is the instrument through which our love is confessed.

All love craves a cross; it measures its love not by the wine it drinks, but by the wine it serves; its greatest jealousy is to be outdone by the cherished rival in the least advantage of self-giving.

And because love is necessarily self-giving and sacrificial, from all eternity God gives Himself in the eternal act of generating His Divine Son, and in time that Divine Son becomes Man and gives His life on a cross for man whom He loves; and the Holy Spirit Who proceeds from Father and Son gives Himself in charity to our hearts that we might be adopted sons of God; and finally we give ourselves to Him Who as the Perfect Love becomes the secret of our eternal happiness.

The love of God in Christ was revealed by His becoming the Man of Sorrows, for if He did not take a cross upon Himself as a proof that He loved us unto death, then the mother who suffers for her children, the soldier who dies for his country, would have shown a greater earthly manifestation of love than the Son of God Himself!

It is from the "Lamb slain from the beginning of the world," and but temporalized on Calvary, that the world derives its inspiration for sacrifice.

Since sacrifice is essential for love, does it not follow that the actors in the drama of suffering are better prepared to understand it?

I say sacrifice, not mere pain or suffering for no one is better because of pain. The difference between pain and sacrifice is love. Suffering without love is pain — sacrifice is suffering with love.

Pain and suffering are from sin and selfishness, but sacrifice is not; it is from love. It is through want of love that pain arises.

Suffering brings one to the door of the Temple; but love is the key that unlocks the door, and by transmuting pain into sacrifice prepares for the happiness of the everlasting dwellings.

Those who have themselves never felt hunger involuntarily through poverty, or voluntarily through fasting, can little understand the legitimate demands of the poor, or the obligation to feed them in charity.

In like manner, those who never have experienced suffering, which can be a condition of love, cannot understand how Cliristian souls resign themselves to Someone who first loved us.

The actors in the drama of suffering understand it better than the spectators, because suffering initiates us into the great mysteries of life.

The spectators only see half the game; they need announcers to explain the plays. The players know the secrets, where they are going and why.

Consider St. Peter for example. He slept in the Garden. This may have been excusable, for up to that point he was only a spectator. He was not yet introduced to the full mystery of the Cross. But he understood the mystery when he himself became an actor in the drama of the Cross.

There is an old legend to the effect that Peter followed the advice of some friends and fled from the terrors of persecution then going on in Rome. A short distance outside the city on the Appian Way, he meets the Risen and Glorified Savior bearing the scars of His Passion. Peter asks: "Quo Vadis Domine" Where art Thou going, O Lord! And the Savior answers: "I am going back again to Rome to be recrucified."

That was enough for Peter. He saw that his own refusal to love the Savior as the Savior loved him, was nailing the Lord again to the Cross.

Back again to Rome he went, and when his hour came to witness to his faith, he, deeming it unworthy to die as the Savior died, asked his executioners to crucify him upside down! And to this day we who venerate his remains in the great Basilica of St. Peter, which stands on the spot where he was crucified — the silent, witness of his 261 successors — read with deep affection the letter he left to us:

"If you suffer anything for justice sake, blessed are you ... it is better, if the will of God should so will, that you suffer for doing good than for doing evil ... in as far as you are partakers of the sufferings of Christ, rejoice" (1 Peter 3:14, 17 and 4:13).

Suffering revealed to Peter the deep mysteries of eternal life, as it does to millions of others. Like fire, it burns away the dross that the fine gold might be ours.

The log in the forest was once only a spectator of the sun's fire; but brought from the forest into the hearth, it becomes now an actor, and returns fire with fire, and sings as it is consumed.

The only recorded time Our Divine Lord ever sang was the night He went out to His death.

So with us our nature is larger than we know, our destiny higher than we know; that is why our higher destinies are best achieved when our lower ends are set at naught.

The silver in the bowels of the earth has a higher destiny than it knows; but only the miners' drill which blasts it from its dark dwelling can assign it to a higher purpose with men.

Plants have a higher destiny than they know; they must therefore be dug up from their roots, and ground between the jaws of death, before they can live in the animal.

Animals have a higher destiny than they know; and only a sacrificial knife can usher them into that higher goal of ministering to the life of man.

Man too has a higher destiny than he knows; but unlike all things below him, he attains it not by self-extinction but by a surrender of the baser part of him, that he may perfect that higher faculty which makes him really a man, a child of God, and an heir of the kingdom of heaven.

The tragedy of life is that when the best is before us, we should choose the less—as Adam chose the fruit in preference to the garden, and the prodigal the husks in preference to the bread. The mystery of life comes only to the actors in the drama:

"I walked a mile with pleasure
    She chattered all the way,
But left me none the wiser
    For all she had to say.

"I walked a mile with sorrow
　And ne'er a word said she,
　But oh, the things I learned from her
　When sorrow walked with me."

Finally, suffering often removes a false sense of values. It makes this problem acute: Are we going forward according to the will of God and every law written in our nature, or are we going to stand alone saving our miserable selfish lives, and in the end lose them?

In great moments of tragedy, sorrow, and pain, we are often given sudden intuitive visions of the utter hollowness and emptiness of life apart from God.

Suffering always begets in us a longing for security; that is why, when the staff of the material upon which we lean pierces our hands, we toss it away and look for a new staff upon which to lean.

So long as husks satisfy, we are not likely to yearn for bread; but once they make hungry where most they satisfy, we seek for new food, new hopes, and new securities.

That is why this war, which manifests the utter stupidity of most modern philosophies of life, and which will empty the barns of those who thought only of filling them, will force souls to seek another security, another hope.

Perhaps men will act now as they did when they were children. Many a child, when reprimanded or punished or denied a wish, will turn away from his present discontent, back to something which once gave him pleasure even though it was only a broken toy.

So too, now that the baubles of a godless world have broken, grown children will seek happiness by turning back to something which gave them happiness in their youth in a moment of sorrow — maybe a prayer they learned at their mother's knee.

Coventry Patmore tells us in a poem how a little boy in sorrow found consolation in clasping bluebells and pennies; so may we draw the moral that, in our present sorrow, it might be well for us to clasp the God Whom we have so long forgotten.

"My little son who look'd from thoughtful eyes
And moved and spoke in quiet grown — up
wise
Having my law the seventh time disobey'd
I struck him and dismiss'd
With hard words, and unkiss'd;
His Mother, who was patient, being dead.

Then fearing lest his grief should hinder sleep
I visited his bed.
But found him slumbering deep
With darken'd eyelids, and their lashes yet
From his late sobbing wet.
And I, with moan
Kissing away his tears, left others of my own;
For on a table drawn beside his head
He had put within his reach
A box of counters and a red-veined stone,
A piece of glass abraded by the beach,
And six or seven shells,
A bottle with bluebells,
And two French copper coins,
ranged there with careful art
To comfort his sad heart."

Perhaps too, in the present sorrow of this
war, we as a nation will go back to the God we
have forgotten and disobeyed, as He in His
goodness consoles us as a Father.

The fundamental difference between the
spectator and the actor is that for the
spectator, man is an ultimate, for the actor,
God is the ultimate; and the spectator is a
spectator because he minds the things of man,
the actor is an actor because he minds the
things of God.

This accounts for these totally different
approaches to the problem of pain and

suffering: The humanitarian spectator wants to alleviate suffering; he will contribute to hospitals, and he will endow universities — but without ever bothering to inquire whether they teach truth or error.

He believes that a day will come when science will do away with men's ills, and that when education is truly universal there will be no more wars.

His responsibility ends by doing something, whether it be giving an ambulance or securing a job for an indigent foreign revolutionary.

If he fails to alleviate suffering, he never worries, for he feels that he has done all that he could; his responsibilities end with his gift. Where he cannot heal, he ignores; whom he cannot relieve, he passes by.

But the actor in the drama of Calvary, on the contrary, begins precisely where the humanitarian leaves off.

He does all the things the humanitarian does, but is very careful when he gives money that it will not be used to destroy life in a hospital, even scientifically, nor ever used to spread error and immorality in schools, however disguised under the cloak of academic freedom.

But he goes beyond this. He seeks to take on the sorrow of his neighbor and to fulfill the injunction of Paul: "Bear one another's burdens" (Gal. 6:2).

The spectator, seeing Christ carrying His Cross to Calvary, would organize a Civil Liberties League and present a protest to Pilate signed by 400 professional signers and then publicize it in the newspapers. But the actor, meeting Christ on the road, would help carry His Cross as Simon did.

The spectator might ask the Savior to lay down His Cross; but the actor will take it up.

The difference between the two is the difference between alleviating and redeeming, between doing all you can, and sharing all you are, for another. The spectator regards trials and sufferings as a problem; the actor regards them as a challenge.

The government is complaining that the people of the United States are too complacent about this war. What is the root of complacency?

It is assuming that we are spectators of the war, rather than actors in it.

If there be national complacency, it is due to a backwash of spiritual complacency.

Peter, James and John slept in the garden of Gethsemane, because they were unmindful of the awfulness of the Savior's Hour. Worry keeps us awake. Therefore these men did not worry. They were blind to the reality of evil at the gates.

And if we be indifferent to danger, may it not be due to the fact that our secular schools for over two generations have been teaching that there is no difference between good and evil; it all depends on your point of view.

Well, if there be no evil, how shall we be aroused to its existence; if there be no goodness how shall we become fired for its defence; if there be no sin and guilt, whence shall come our moral indignation?

Now that a war is upon us, we must begin to realize that we are not spectators of reality, but actors. As we plunge into the sacrifice, blood, sweat and toil of war, we must be stirred to a sense of corporate responsibility to our fellowmen and the world.

Prayer and adoration must awaken our national conscience, for the whole world is in a mess because of sin — and the sin of all of us,

in varying degrees: the sin of forgetting God
and His Divine Son.

Since sin is a common debt, let none of us
ask to be exempt from that burden. Each Holy
Hour must be made, not for our particular
intention, but to pay off some debt of the
world's sin and to restore the world once again
to the reign of God's moral law and the
Kingship of His Divine Son.

The ledger of the world reveals a
tremendous moral debt. Each time we make
an Hour we scratch off some of that debt, we
draw the world farther away from hate and
closer to the mercy of God.

We thus become actors in the drama of
restoring the world to sanity, for presently it
has gone mad! The whole world is in the state
of mortal sin! It needs redemption.

This Holy Hour is not alone to atone for
these sins, it is also to assure the future. It
has no political significance; it appeals only to
Jews, Protestants, and Catholics who believe
they are more than beasts that eat, drink, and
die; it will not appeal to weaklings, but only to
heroes.

It has no economic or political plans
because it seeks not to create a good society;

but it does seek to create the creators of a good society.

America is not yet conscious of the necessity of sacrifice and a cross. We are flying from it as Peter did — unable to understand how sacrifice, as conditioned by love, brings life and restores a true sense of values.

And the Lord is meeting America on the roadway of life, asking us the question Peter asked: "Quo Vadis, America" — Where are you going America? That's it! Where are we going!

Are we going to the Cross as spectators or as Actors? What is your answer? As the majority in America answer so shall be the future of America.

THE DIVINE COST OF
STOPPING THIS WAR

In this chapter, we enter into the very heart of the question: "Why does God not stop the war?" The answer is to be found in another question, namely: "What would be the divine cost of stopping this war?" The answer is, God would have to destroy human freedom.

This needs some explanation. Let us begin with this fact: That this is not the only kind of world God could have made. He could have made a world without freedom.

He could have so fashioned us that we would have been good with the same necessity with which the sun rises in the east and sets in the west. We might all have been saintly with the same necessity, with which the lily is white, or fire is hot, or ice is cold.

But God willed not to make a mechanical universe, peopled by automata; rather did He choose to communicate to us something of Himself, namely His Freedom — not in the same degree of perfection, of course, but enough of it to say a "no" which would give charm to a "yes," when we freely chose to say it.

In other words, God chose to make a moral universe, where characters would emerge by the right use of freedom — a universe where there would be patriots because men might be traitors; a universe like a nation, like a battlefield, where there would be heroes because men might be cowards; a universe like the Church, where there would be saints because men might also be devils.

There is no epic for the certainties of life and no lyric without the suspense of sorrow and the sigh of fear; no watchful love hovers over the invulnerable, nor crown of merit rests suspended over those who do not fight.

Take this quality of freedom away from man and there would be no more reason to honor the fortitude of martyrs and soldiers than to honor the flames or the bullets which sent them to their death.

God willed to make a moral universe of praise and blame, but this could be done only by making men captains and masters of their own fate and destiny.

There is one word which sums up God's plan in making the universe, and that is love.

God made each heart capable of love. But love implies a choice.

A heart that loves must be a heart to give or to keep. Because, therefore, God willed to make us, so we could love Him in this world, He had to make us free; but if He made us free to love, He had to make it possible for us to be free to hate.

The universe thus became populated with free wills, little gods, each armed with a reflection of God's freedom.

That some of these little gods would will wrongly was inevitable, for they had not God's Wisdom; that some of them would be rebellious was inevitable, for, being free, they could make a false declaration of independence and become like little foolish rays of the sun attempting to make themselves independent of the sun.

The fact that we come from God would not necessarily dispense us from the evil effects of such rebellion, any more than because a child is the son of a King he is immune from drowning if he disobeys and goes into the whirlpool.

God gave us the power to rebel that there might be meaning and honor in our allegiance when we freely choose to give it.

God pledged Himself, after giving us that freedom, never to destroy it, regardless of how many petulant souls would shriek against Him: "Why does God not stop the war?"

God could challenge us, overrule us, permit us to be visited by the consequences of our misdeeds — but He would never destroy that great gift of freedom.

Man could, if he so wanted, go on defying God for all time and eternity, subvert His moral law, blast the cosmos, and even break His Heart, but still God would not take away our freedom.

In this sense the Decree of Creation to make man free was also the decree of Calvary, for a free man that could break his commandment could also crucify Him.

Not even then would God destroy human freedom; but in His Goodness He would make man's misuse of freedom the felix culpa, the occasion of offering Himself as a holocaust of love, not to force men back to Him, for His hands and feet were nailed, but to entice them back by a revelation of love greater than which no man hath — that he lay down his life for a friend.

This brings us to the question: "Could God stop the war?"

Most certainly! But if God were ever to be untrue to Himself or to us, what would God have to do? He would have to destroy our freedom! That would be the divine cost of stopping this war.

We say we are fighting for freedom? Then why do we ask God to destroy freedom — and that is precisely what we demand in asking: "Why does God not stop the war?"

We say we are fighting to destroy dictators. Then why do we ask God to become a dictator? We say that dictators are wicked because they would destroy the last vestige of freedom on earth. Then why do we ask for a Dictator in heaven?

Shall we one moment rage against earthly dictators because they trample liberty underfoot, and in the next moment shriek for a Dictator in the Heaven Who will do the same thing?

Certainly, if we had to choose, it would be far better to live under earthly dictators for a few years than to have a Dictator in heaven who, by one blast of omnipotent power, would take away that quality in us that makes us the paragons of creation.

Fortunately, however, we have no choice in the matter. God will not destroy freedom; He will not be a Dictator. And that is why God will not stop the war.

Where then should the blame of war be placed: On God's gift of freedom, or on our abuse of freedom?

Have we not been too proud to admit we might be sinful? When the world goes wrong, we blame it on systems, tyrannies, governments, unsound economics, or bad glands but never on our own will.

Would we know how much the modern world has abused freedom, then cast a glance at the two false theories of Liberalism and Totalitarianism.

Liberalism defines freedom as the right to do whatever you please, and that is the way freedom is understood by 90% of young Americans educated in non-religious institutions. If freedom means that, it means anarchy.

Freedom thus becomes a physical power, not a moral power; an absence of law instead of a respect for it; a right without a corresponding duty; a license without responsibility.

Totalitarianism on the other hand defines freedom as a duty to do what you must. If freedom means that, it means tyranny.

Freedom thus becomes a duty without a right and comes into being only when the individual will identifies itself with the will of the dictator.

Under this system there is no will but the class will or the national will or the race will. The person no longer exists.

Let loose false concepts of freedom like that in the world and you cannot stop war. The first abuse of freedom which identifies it with absence of law or self-expression, creates war through conflicting egotisms; the second abuse of freedom which identifies it with the will of the dictator, begets war through force and violence.

That is not the kind of freedom God gave us; that is the way we distorted it.

True freedom does not mean the right to do whatever you please, nor the duty to do whatever you must; but it means the right to do whatever you ought — and oughtness implies law, responsibility, purpose. In other words, freedom is inseparable from the God of Love Who made us.

As the pendulum is most free to swing when it has a fixed point of suspension, so we are most free when we are rooted in the Law and the Love of the God Who made us. And that is what Our Divine Lord meant when He said: "The truth shall make you free" (John 8:32).

Our Declaration of Independence affirms that liberty is an "unalienable" right, because a gift of the Creator. In other words, it makes us independent of tyrannies and dictators by making a Declaration of Dependence on God.

The real evil in the human situation, then, lies in man's unwillingness to recognize his finiteness, his creaturehood, or the possibility that there exists something greater than himself.

All pride, vanity, sensuality, cruelty, force, and licentiousness originate in man's denial that freedom is a gift, through which he seeks

to give himself the appearance of
unconditioned reality.

The sin of man is that he makes himself
God, as St. Paul says: "For the wrath of God is
revealed from heaven against all ungodliness
and wickedness of those men who in
wickedness hold back the truth of God, seeing
that what may be known about God is
manifest to them. For God has manifested it to
them. For since the creation of the world His
invisible attributes are clearly seen — His
everlasting power also and divinity — being
understood through the things that are made.
And so they are without excuse, seeing, that,
although they knew God, they did not glorify
Him as God or give thanks, but became vain
in their reasonings, and their senseless minds
have been darkened" (Rom. 1:18-23).

Sin is the abuse of freedom; that is why the
modern man, who denied sin, found himself in
a world of dictatorship.

Even the idea of hell is bound up with
freedom because hell means abuse of
responsibility. Deny hell and you deny
responsibility; deny responsibility and you
deny freedom.

We began this chapter with the question:
"Why does God not stop the war?" Now the

question is turned around? Why do we not stop warring against God?

This war is not of God's arbitrary making; it is the effect of our abuse of God's gift of freedom. We must therefore not expect God to suspend the operation of His laws to protect us from their consequences.

God will not suspend the law of gravitation to protect the life of a man who violates the "oughtness" of his free life by throwing himself off the Empire State Building. Neither will God suspend the operation of His moral law to immunize man from a war born of the abuse of freedom and the "de-Christianisation of individual and social life."

We have a war to win for the sake of peace with justice in the world. Apart from the economic, military, and political considerations, necessary for victory, there should be a moral quality underlying them all, namely, humility.

Let us not think of dictators as the creators of the world's woe; but rather as its creatures.

These dictators are like boils, superficial manifestations of an inner rottenness. They would never have come to the surface if there had not been the proper conditions in the world from which they came.

It would therefore be a fatal mistake to think that if we got rid of them, the world would be lovely and rosy. In the last World War we made that very mistake.

We assumed that if we could get rid of the Kaiser, the world would once more live in peace and prosperity. Well, we defeated the Kaiser: but we have another World War in 21 years.

We removed the boil, but we kept the infected bad blood; we rid ourselves of the symbol of the world's wrong, but we did nothing to correct the wrong.

What assurance have we now that if we defeat these wicked dictators, the world will pursue justice and righteousness? Unless we cut down the evil tree that begets this evil fruit, we shall have to go on having more wars.

To change the figure, it will do no good to treat the world for fox-bite if, like the Spartan youth, it is going to carry a fox in its blouse.

This war is really only an episode in the working out of a great truth; it is not the great truth that is an episode of the war. And that

51

truth is that this war is not a sign that men are with God, but a sign that they have been against Him.

What I am trying to say is, God did not start this war and God will not stop it apart from our free cooperation with His Law, which is the perfection of our freedom.

Let us stop thinking of our woes and sorrows and wars as having been thrust upon us by systems and dictators, but rather as being the effects of the evil rebellion against God.

When the world is crashing down on our heads it is no time to say that the major frustrations of life are economic or political, or that if there were another system of economics or another system of government all would be well. It is not the systems of the world that have gone crazy, but the hearts.

Economics and politics upset the world because evil and selfishness and godlessness first upset the hearts of economists and dictators.

To assure ourselves that the major ills of our times are not economic, we need but inquire into who are the disillusioned people of the modern world. They are those who possess, who have power, who are selfish and satiated, who need blaring orchestras without melodies to drown their self-consciousness.

There is a thousand times more disenchantment among the intelligentsia than among the proletariat. Something else is wrong, then, besides the economics: Our souls have lost God.

From a Christian point of view, there has been a forgetfulness and an outlawry of God's Divine Son from the hearts of men and the society of nations.

As in the days of His physical life, He did not bring a cross into this world, but found it here, made by the sin and evil of men; so in these days of His Mystical Presence on earth in His Church, He finds another cross, made from the distortion of His gift of freedom: Our wills set against His. No wonder the cross is a contradiction of one bar with another.

We should enter into a national act of reparation and prayer humbly, as Our Lord entered the Garden of Gethsemane. Innocent though He was, He took upon Himself the sins of the world, as if that burden were His own; in the strong language of Scripture was "made sin."

So should we enter this war, not regarding ourselves as innocent victims of others sins for we are all sinners — but as transgressors assuming part of the blame for the sins of the world.

If there is anyone who thinks he is good, let him realize that he lives in an evil world and therefore must redeem it; if, however, we feel ourselves as guilty, because we abused God's freedom, then we have need of making atonement for ourselves.

In either case, we are under God's purposes, humbly submitting ourselves to His Will either to repair the broken fences of our neighbors, or to replant our own wrecked vineyards.

Like unto the Master in the Garden, we will never admit we are under a violence imposed by men, but under the sweet compulsion of furthering the cause of God.

In our hearts, we will feel less that we are suffering from man's injustices than from a free cooperation with God's justice for the Redemption of the world.

When evil men came with swords and clubs to apprehend Him in the Garden, He might have said: "This is your hour and power of darkness — your hour of darkness. All you can do with it is to turn out the light, to spread darkness over the world. Evil has its hour."

Evil has its hour now and we are in darkness. No wonder the Savior, when that Hour was up, went to His Apostles and said: "Couldst thou not watch one hour?" (Mark 14:37). In other words, we must meet the hour of darkness with the hour of watching!

TRUST IN GOD'S PLAN

The mere fact that we ask the question: "Why does God permit this war," is in itself an indication of want of trust in either the Wisdom or the Goodness of God.

How explain this want of trust? Generally, it is due to a refusal to admit: First, the possibility that God knows more than I and is better than l; and secondly, that my dignity is not lowered by submitting to His Wisdom and His Goodness even when they go against me.

Though the great mass of people who ignore God never state their religious perplexities in these simple terms, they are nevertheless the basic reasons why God is exiled from human hearts, from the family, and from our national life.

Pride is at the root of it all; a pride of intellect and pride of will which makes man frame a universe of which lie, and not God, is the center. Pride has its roots in a false declaration of independence, namely a refusal to recognize that man is not the author of his own existence.

The ultimate manifestation of pride is self-deification: Setting oneself up as God. That is why the intellectually proud man will attempt to convince you of his omniscience; he steals the mantle of God's wisdom and drapes it about his own shoulders.

His favorite trick in conversation is to make you think he knows everything.

The result is that today we have information, but not wisdom. Information is uncorrelated bits of knowledge which, like a broken egg, can never be composed into a complete philosophy of life. Wisdom, on the contrary, is a knowledge of truth, human and divine.

Information and quiz programs have indoctrinated us into believing that the man who knows the colors of the three beards mentioned in Hamlet is wise; or who can tell what four novelists of the Victorian era wrote about oysters on the half-shell, is wise; and that if we do not know similar patches of information, we ought to dissolve into an emotional crumble.

True wisdom, on the contrary, correlates information into causes, and equips itself to answer such basic questions as: "What is the purpose of life?" "Why are we here and where are we going?"

A little child who knows the first page of his catechism which sums up the wisdom of Aristotle and the best thinking of Western culture, knows more than all the university professors who define religion, including an Ohio professor who expresses his thought on this matter as "the projection into the roaring loom of time of a unified complex of psychical values" — whatever that means!

Our Divine Lord implied that much in inveighing against crazy quilt information, when if we may paraphrase His words, He said: "O Heavenly Father, I thank Thee that Thou hast hidden these things from the university professors and the experts and revealed them to the little ones."

The salvation of modern man lies not in a pride of what he knows, but in a humility concerning how little he knows. His omniscience must give way to nescience; instead of feeling he knows everything, he must come closer to the truth that he really knows nothing.

His belief that he knows all must surrender to the humiliating truth that someone is wiser than he. For if man knows all, how can God teach him anything?

If there is no law above him, how can he ever do wrong? If the mind is filled with self how fill it with Divine Wisdom? For not until we become humble can there be trust.

For an illustration of this, turn to the book of Job. "There was a man in the land of Hus, whose name was Job, and that man was simple and upright, and fearing God, and avoiding evil" (Job 1:1).

As the story is unfolded, Job was gradually divested of all the things that clothe the spirit of a man, those things on which a man leans for help and strength.

First he lost his wealth, then he lost his children, seven sons and three daughters; next, his health; then the love and consolation of his wife, who said to him: "Dost thou still continue in thy simplicity? Bless God and die." To which Job answered: "Thou hast spoken like one of the foolish women: if we have received good things at the hands of God, why should we not receive evil?" (Job 2:9, 10).

We now see the naked spirit of the man. There were only two things that were left: God and himself. God, he never denied: himself he could not escape.

But between God and himself there seemed to be no place of meeting, no reconciliation, for here was a man who was suffering — but not because he had done wrong.

Like millions of innocents, through the ages, who have done no wrong and yet suffer, Job at first did not understand the ultimate meaning of the agony that gripped his heart.

His intellect was confronted with a problem too great for his little mind, as from his lips there came a string of "Whys."

"Why did I not die in the womb, why did I not perish when I came out of the belly? Why received upon the knees? Why suckled at the breasts?" (Job 3:11, 12). "Have I not dissembled? have I not kept silence? have I not been quiet? and indignation is come upon me." (Job 3:26). "Why is light given to him that is in misery, and life to them that are in bitterness of soul?" (Job 3:20).

Three comforters came to console Job. One of them, Eliphaz, attempted to account for the suffering of Job on the ground that it must be the result of personal sin; his theory was that it is only the wicked who suffer. "Is it a great matter that God should comfort thee? but thy wicked words hinder this" (Job 15:11).

Job protested his innocence, but Eliphaz insisted that Job must be guilty of many crimes, and promised him prosperity if he would repent. "If thou wilt return to the Almighty thou shalt be built up, and shalt put away iniquity far from thy tabernacle" (Job 22:23).

Another of Job's comforters, Elihu by name, who talked like a university professor who never understood his philosophy well enough to tell it in simple language, began a long speech on the justice and power of God.

Never before in the history of the world was any speech cut short more abruptly, for it was not man but God Who broke in on his intellectual droolings, and out of the whirlwind asked: "Who is this that wrappeth up sentences in unskillful words?" (Job 38:2).

How would we feel as we sat alongside the bed of a sick friend, offering him the consolation of our great wisdom, to have God cut short our consolation by driving us into nescience.

Now that God appears on the scene, should we not expect an answer to the questions Job asked?

Certainly if a Broadway dramatist were putting on this play, he would have God step onto the stage and solve all the problems of evil and answer all the questions of Job, or else ring np a cash register and give away a gold mine.

Everything in the universe would click; there would be no loose edges; we would know all when we left the theatre.

But the God of Heaven's Way does not do things like the god of Broadway.

When the true God appeared on the stage, what does He do? Here was the Supreme Expert on the Supreme Quiz Program! Information please? And God was there to give it!

But lo and behold! Instead of answering the questions of Job He begins to ask Job questions; instead of giving information, He dispensed wisdom.

And this is how He began: "Gird up thy loins like a man: I will ask thee, and answer thou me.

'Where wert thou when I laid the
foundations of the earth? tell me if thou hast
understanding.

'Who hath laid the measures thereof, if
thou knowest? or who hath stretched the line
upon it?

'Upon what are its bases grounded? or who
laid the cornerstone thereof?

'Who shut up the sea with doors, when it
broke forth as issuing out of the womb?

'When I made a cloud the garment thereof,
and wrapped it in a mist as in swaddling
bands? ... Hast thou entered into the depths of
the sea, and walked in the lowest parts of the
deep?

'Have the gates of death been opened to
thee, and hast thou seen the darksome doors?

'Hast thou considered the breadth of the
earth? tell me, if thou knowest all things?

'Where is the way where light dwelleth, and
where is the place of darkness?... Didst thou
know then that thou shouldst be born? and
didst thou know the number of thy days?

'Hast thou entered into the storehouses of the snow, or hast thou beheld the treasures of the hail?... Who is the father of rain? or who begot the drops of dew?

"Out of whose womb came the ice; and the frost from heaven who hath gendered it? ... Shalt thou be able to join together the shining stars the Pleiades, or canst thou stop the turning about of Arcturus?

"Canst thou bring forth the day star in its time, and make the evening star to rise upon the children of the earth?

'Dost thou know the order of heaven, and canst thou set down the reason thereof on the earth? ... Canst thou lift up thy voice to the clouds, that an abundance of waters may cover thee? ... Who hath put wisdom in the heart of man? or who gave the cock understanding? ... Will the eagle mount up at thy command, and make her nest in high places? ... Shall he that contendeth with God be so easily silenced? surely he that reproveth God, ought to answer r him." (Job 38:3 to 39:33).

In that whole speech of God, no reference was made to the suffering of Job; no explanation was offered of anything that had transpired.

But God did one thing: He brought Job face to face with the universe in which he lived; asked him if he were equal to creating it, to governing it even to the fall of a sparrow, and made him see that he was a small part of a vast and mighty whole.

And when God finished asking Job questions Job realized that the questions of God were more satisfying than the answers of men; that the true nescience into whose abyss he was driven was really the beginning of wisdom.

Job now saw that he had been asking only one question: How could his individual problem be solved? And God's answer was, that his question was but one of a million others, for he lived among men and things and until he could understand the answers to those million questions, he could never understand the answer to that one.

Job saw too that God's words contained the audacious indictment that he must take his eyes off himself, for he had been too self-absorbed; he must understand the limitations of his own knowledge; he must trust in God because God knows all and wills what is best for all and for each.

Where would trust be if we understood everything? Where would faith be if there were nowhere complexity? Where would love be, if there were no confidence? By driving Job back into nescience God laid the foundation of trust.

And in the light of that unveiling there came to Job a discovery of himself by comparison.

No more did he ask the why of suffering; he saw that he could still accept it and be sure of God; that he could believe in God's Righteousness when everything God did seemed to be denying it; that evil fits into the divine good of the world; that even death can be God's servant carrying out God's mysterious ends and purposes, within the limits of the divine permission.

In the agony of war we too must realize that in the divine plan evil may be momentarily victorious, but in the total process it always loses.

Sin may win the booty but it loses the battle, as the devil lost the battle with Job and Job regained more than he lost.

The omnipotence of God does not mean that everything that happens is His Will; it means that nothing that happens can defeat His Will.

Being all-powerful He can allow evil its brief hour for a more ultimate good.

"Let both grow together until the harvest; and at harvest time I will say to the reapers, Gather up first the weeds, and bind them in bundles to burn; but the wheat gather into my barn" (Matt. 13:30).

God would not permit anything to happen that had the power of, and by itself, to separate us from Him.

And in the seeming chaos of war and disorder, God still attaches an eternal value to each individual soul.

"Are not two sparrows sold for a farthing?

And yet not one of them will fall to the ground without your Father's leave. But as for you, the very hairs of your head are all numbered. Therefore, do not be afraid; you are of more value than many sparrows" (Matt. 10:29-31).

If the Kingdom of God not only got over the murder of Christ, but made it the great instrument of Redemption, then there is nothing that it cannot get over, and nothing that it cannot turn into an eternal blessing to the glory of His Holy Name.

We do not always understand this plan, because, like Job, we may not understand how our own individual problems fit into it in a general way.

It is easy for us to fall into the error of thinking that the laws of the universe should be suspended or interrupted every time a good man gets in trouble.

If the business of religion was merely to get the religious out of trouble, religion would then cease to be religion; it would become a kind of gigantic insurance policy, which would be the end of religion for the simple reason that it would be faithless.

A mouse that crawls into a grand piano and has its gnawing of the keys disturbed by a great artist entertaining an audience with a Mozart or a Chopin, must in its own puny little brain think that the universe is without a plan.

The spider which weaves its web on the girder of a great steel beam that is lifted into a bridge cannot possibly understand how its own little plan for catching flies must give way

to the engineer's greater plans for
transportation.

So neither can our minds, given to
selfishness and the pursuit of immediate
interests, understand how the omnipotent all-
wise God of the Heavens works out all things
to that which is best for our salvation, and the
triumph of Truth and Goodness.

Tapestries are woven not from the front,
but from the back, and it is only when the last
thread is drawn that we see the completed
design. As Father Tabb has put it:

"My life is but a weaving
   Between my God and me
   I may but choose the colors
   He worketh skillfully

"Full oft He chooses sorrow
   And I, in foolish pride
   Forget He sees the upper
   And I, the under side."

We must be paient and trust in God's plan.
What makes it difficult is that we are always
in a hurry; God is not. Our Divine Lord seems
to suggest that the cvil things are done in a
hurry.

To betraying Judas he said: "What thou dost, do quickly" (John 13:27); and of an impetuous man, he asked, "But which of you by being anxious about it can add to his stature a single cubit?" (Luke 12:25).

Our precipitancy very likely may make us distort the fundamental issues involved. We are very apt to be like James and John on the occasion of Our Savior's visit to the Samaritans, who rejected Him because His face was set towards the Cross.

These two brothers, whom Our Lord called Boanerges, or Sons of Thunder, were impatient for revenge and asked that God send lightning to burn their villages.

It seemed fitting that the Sons of Thunder should ask for lightning. But Our Lord said: "You do not know of what manner of spirit you are; for the Son of Man did not come to destroy men's lives, but to save them" (Luke 9:55-56).

Such is the spirit of the Cross. The spirit that wants to call down fire upon those that are refusing Jesus Christ is the spirit of evil; it lacks the principle of the Cross.

James and John lacked patience; the Divine Savior was willing to suffer the insults of the Samaritans for a moment, in order that He might win their souls later on.

And His patience was rewarded, for one of the very first cities in which the Gospel was preached was the city of the Samaritans. And it was from a Samaritan village that there came forth for the first time in the hearing of men the expression, "Savior of the world."

In the parable of the man who sowed a field of wheat and who had it spoiled by the enemy sowing weeds among the wheat, the servants of the householder came to him and said: "Sir didst thou not sow good seed in thy field, how then does it have weeds?" He said to them:

"An enemy hath done this." And the servant said to him: "Wilt thou have us to go and gather them up." "No," he said, "lest in gathering the weeds, you root up the wheat along with it. Let both grow together until the harvest; and at harvest time I will say to the reaper, Gather up first the weeds and bind them into bundles to burn, but the wheat gather into my barn" (Matt. 13:24-31).

Many of us are like the servants, who would want the evil to be rooted up immediately. But the Savior is more patient.

Let both grow until the harvest. Let these two sowings work themselves out to the final manifestation, and then there will be a separation.

The harvest of the sons of the Kingdom will be a harvest of sunlight upon the world. The harvest of the sons of evil will be one of evil, of things which offend and defile, and His reapers will at last gather them up and cast them into the final burning.

What then shall be our attitude? Trust in God while abiding in His will!

Writing to the Thessalonians, St. Paul said: "May the Lord direct your hearts into the love of God and the patience of Christ" (2 Thes. 3:5).

We live in the midst of evil days it is true, but it is not because God is not good; it is because we have not been good.

About one third of the civilized world crucified Him, and another third abandoned Him, and the other third while living good lives as individuals have not had enough influence to affect the political, economic, and moral life in which they lived.

This war, let us be sure about it, is not for "freedom" any more than the last war was for "democracy."

It is a gigantic struggle to decide whether in the next few centuries we shall live by the moral law rooted in God or in the law of force rooted in Satan.

Whether we know it or not, we are fighting for a moral order, not because we willed it in God, but because our enemies, thank God, have forced us into that position.

It may take some time before we realize the greatness of our cause — we may first have to lose much of what we have; but let it not be said that while unconsciously fighting for a morality rooted in God, we consciously abandoned trust in God Who alone can save.

Guns and bullets alone will not win this war. We need them — certainly. But we need more a realization that some of our enemies have the devil on their side and man is no match for the devil.

That is why we will either return to God or we will perish. And by returning to God I mean: First, that we ground our law in the authority of God; Second, that we make economics a branch of ethics, and third, that we base family life on the moral law.

This cannot be accomplished by legislative enactments, publicity campaigns, or radio appeals. Neither can it be done by retreating from the world's harsh conflicts into individual prayerful isolation.

It can be accomplished only by the prayerful minded citizens of the United States realizing that they are signed with the social sign of the Cross, and that when they pray, like Our Divine Lord, they take humanity with them even the humanity of their enemies.

We live in an age where indifference to God and the moral law on the part of economics and politics, has led to an invasion of the soul by economics and politics. Such is the meaning of totalitarianism.

How shall due order be restored except by a vast army of believers in God and His Divine Son creating a new public opinion with social implications of a revolutionary character, whereby we will render to God the things that are God's.

Lose not then your trust in God. Be humble. He has not failed; We have failed:

This is the time of probation! Trust in God while abiding in His Will!

In the language of St. Paul: "And may the Lord direct your hearts into the love of God and the patience of Christ" (2 Thess. 3:5).

When you go to a mystery play, do you walk out in the first act, because one of the good characters is killed, or because evil is momentarily victorious? Do you judge the play by the first few lines?

If you believe the dramatist has a plot, why not give God credit for a plot?

Perhaps this war so far is only the first scene of the first act, as we witness the bitter fruits of our complacency and the onward march of our enemies.

We may have to sit through a few more acts before we become wise like the Prodigal, or before we become humble.

Patience, then! "He that would have a cake out of wheat, must tarry the grinding." What wound ever healed, except by degrees? And our world is wounded.

Give up your faith in everything else if you must, in credit, mass — production; wealth;

but surrender not your faith in Him Who alone
can save:

"My soul, sit then a patient looker on,
Judge not the play   before the play is done,
The plot hath many changes every day.
Speak a new scene; the last act crowns a
play."

FAITH IN WAR TIME

In all crises and in particular in time of war we must not worry about getting God on our side; we must worry about getting on God's side.

Before this war began some so — called leaders who lived by Christianity instead of for it, spent their time adjusting Christianity to the way people lived, rather than adjusting the way they lived to Christianity.

When divorce became common they dropped the words of Our Lord, "What therefore God has joined together, let no man put asunder" (Matt. 19:6). When sin abounded, they called sin a myth and hell an illusion.

The modern mind thus became accustomed to adjust creed to life rather than life to creed. If medicine followed similar tactics and accommodated itself to disease, because it is common, society long ago would have been prostrate.

We must be careful not to transplant that false peace-time mentality to war-times.

Just as in times of peace some men thought it was the business of God and Christianity to make the world comfortable — whether or not men were doing the will of God — so now, when war comes, these same individuals assume that Christianity exists either to buttress up an order that has outlawed Christ from individual and social life, or else to validate our national slogans.

God, then, is judged to be good, if He does our will; He is judged to be weak and cruel if He refuses to do it.

If religion is to bring any consolation in time of war, we must talk less about whether God is on our side, and more about whether we are on God's side.

When a husband and wife are quarreling, the true problem is not how to fit their selfishness into the Sermon on the Mount, but rather how to fit the Sermon on the Mount into their quarrel.

The clay does not mold the potter, but the potter the clay. In like manner, we are not to attempt to fit Christianity into this war, but to fit this war into Christianity.

Patriotism is a part of religion, but religion is not a part of patriotism. Caesar is under God, but God is not under Caesar.

To love God is necessarily to love one's country, but to love one's country is not necessarily to love God.

Goodness is in the will, not in slogans; in persons, not in processes; in souls, not in catchwords.

The idea that God can be used for any purpose, is magic; it is not religion. The modern attempt of some to make Christianity fit this war in its entirety is really the renewal of the Crucifixion, where men attempted to make the Son of God fit something else they had made: the Cross.

As then they patterned the Son of God to a cross, so now they would pattern Him to a war. To nail the Son of God to our ideologies and ways of thinking is the greatest tragedy of the world. For if God is not above our righteousness, but is identical with it, then why bother with God at all?

If God hates those whom we hate, then who shall forgive them their sins, and how shall we be pardoned our late? What I am trying to say in a clumsy way, is what Isaias

said so clearly in one line: "For my thoughts
are not your thoughts: nor your ways my
ways, saith the Lord" (Isaias 55:8).

Why, it may be asked, should we be less
interested in getting God on our side, and
more interested in getting on God's side?
Because that is the only way really to insure
victory.

But why is identification with God's will the
path to victory? Because God's purposes are
always preserved from defeat by the very
nature of things.

Good is self-conserving; evil is self-
defeating. Evil is unstable, because it is
contrary to the nature of things.

Excessive eating, excessive drinking, or
excessive exercise is contrary to the nature of
the body and in the end injures it. Obedience
to the laws of hygiene, on the contrary,
conserves us in health; rebellion against them
begets disease.

How many of us would take the proper care
of health if the violation of its laws did not
bring a penalty?

There are laws written in the cosmos,
across the face of the skies, in the chemicals,

plants, and animals, in our bodies and minds, and they are all reflections of the Eternal Reason of Almighty God.

We are free, of course, to break any of God's laws; but in breaking them we defeat ourselves. We are free to defy the law of gravitation; but in doing so, we do not destroy gravitation, we destroy ourselves.

The Prodigal was free to leave the Father's house, but in doing so, he defeated not the Father, but himself.

Judas did not sell the Master for thirty pieces of silver; he sold himself. Judas perished; Christ lives on. Good is self-conserving; evil is self-defeating.

There is no need for God to intervene to frustrate the evil purposes of men who ignore the moral law, for men cannot be in opposition to Him without being in opposition to themselves.

The confusions created by our rejection of God are not determined by our intentions, but by the nature of the Reality we negate, namely God. However good my intention may be in holding my hand over fire, my hand will nevertheless be burned.

Nature belongs to God, not to us. That is why it betrays us, but never betrays Him. That is why nature turns against us and punishes us, when we do not use it rationally or as God intended. As Francis Thompson put it:

I tempted all His servitors, but to find
My own betrayal in their constancy,
In faith to Him their fickleness to me,
Their traitorous trueness, and their loyal deceit.

We are punished on earth by the very things we distrust from God's purposes; in this sense: "the wages of sin is death" (Rom. 6:23).

The scriptures tell us: "And he who falls on this stone will be broken to pieces; but upon whomever it falls, it will grind him to powder" (Matt. 21:44). In other words, anyone who opposes Christ shall be crushed; it will not be Christ who shall be crushed.

When Nazism and Communism persecute religion they seal their own doom, not the doom of religion. As the Spanish proverb puts it: "He who spits against heaven spits in his own face."

The universe absolutely will not respond to anti-Christian living. Everything from the stars to the earth on which we live will rebel against a denial of God's law. The divine plan never fails, for the stone which the builders rejected is made the head of the corner."

Julian the Apostate found it out when he ran a dagger into his breast, shrieking: "O Galilean, Thou hast conquered."

Since God's purposes are never defeated, it follows that to the extent that our purposes are identical with His, we can never lose. There can be no such thing as fearing their evil if we be on God's side.

Our Lord never once said, "Fear the devil." But He did say, "Fear God" (1 Pet. 2:17). If our enemies are evil, we should fear less being defeated by them, than we should fear defeating ourselves, by forgetfulness of God and His Divine Son.

Evil may be triumphant for a moment, but it is always deprived of the results of its triumphs; it wins the first battle, but it always loses the booty. God's purpose prevails.

Caesar built roads to carry the screaming eagles of militarism throughout the world, but over these same roads Peter and Paul walked to preach the good tidings of the Gospel of Christ.

Rome built temples of marble to the pagan gods; the same marble was shaped into tabernacles for the worship of the Eucharistic Lord.

Unless our resolves be in accord with God, we can never be assured of victory. But if they are in accordance with the Divine Will, then we shall have His victory; for Our Divine Lord said "I have overcome the world" (John 16:33).

His law, His life, and His truth will win therefore, whether we win or lose, because goodness is self-conserving.

If therefore we remain with Him, victory will be ours, though at any one moment it may look like defeat, feel like defeat, and smell like defeat. The Cross looked like defeat too, but it was the condition of His greatest victory.

Wherein lies America's assurance of victory? In the correspondence of our wills to His natural law, to His moral law, to His Christian love for "If God is for us, who is against us" (Rom. 8:31). As Our Divine Lord Himself told us: "Without me you can do nothing" (John 15:5).

If God is eternally the God Who is crucified in the tragedies of history, so is He forever and eternally the God Who raised Jesus from the

Dead. That is why faith in Him can triumph over all disaster.

But the condition of that triumph is oneness with Him. Hence this importance of an all-out moral effort, involving a return to the Christian concept of family life, and the acceptance of a system of law grounded on the authority of God and a system of education based on prayer and love of God.

We must remember that in war two factors must be considered: 1) arms; and 2) the courage with which they are used.

The initial success of the totalitarian armies lies not only in their military equipment, but principally because they used it with a religious enthusiasm — not with the fire of a true faith, but with the fire of a false one. They were fighting for an absolute, a deity, a philosophy of life.

America can match them in arms. But shall we match them in that imponderable factor of morale? Can their faith in the absolute of a false god be matched by our moral relativity, our indifference to God, His moral law, and the Redemption of His Divine Son?

Can the flames of their fanaticism be extinguished by the gentle zephyrs of our indifference, which denies there is any distinction between good and evil?

Can their zeal for anti-Christ be overcome by our indifference to Christ? Can their inspiration for sacrifice born of devotion to their false absolute, be matched by our emphasis on a false freedom which thinks that every appeal for sacrifice is a violation of constitutional rights, or property rights, or the right to organize?

We are united so far because we have a common hate; but where is our common love? Shall we be "united nations" only because we hate the same devil, or because we all love the same God?

This war so far has not provided us with a national slogan, probably because the last war taught us that slogans are dangerous. Twenty years ago we shouted: "Make the world safe for democracy" and all we did was to make it unsafe for democracy.

Occasionally a slogan is used today that we are fighting for freedom. But this has not been popular, because the people who think know that freedom from something is meaningless unless we are free for something — and that objective has not been defined.

Freedom is like the atmosphere; it is a condition of happy living, but it is not the purpose of life. We want freedom from slavery, but we do not want a freedom so broad as to include the right to destroy it.

Slogans are useful in time of peace, but not in time of war; for a slogan is a myth, a catchword to awaken mass enthusiasm.

Today people want a philosophy of life, a true absolute to knock down the false absolute, and a faith for war time.

We already have the negative side of that faith; that is, that our enemies have an evil philosophy of life that makes civilization impossible. We have not yet developed a positive philosophy, namely that that evil can be overcome only by good.

No one wants an American victory more than I do; I am just realistic about it, for history attests the truth of David: "Unless the Lord build the house, they labour in vain that build it. Unless the Lord keep the city, he watcheth in vain that keepeth it" (Ps. 126-1).

Victory will come if we arouse ourselves to a sense of duty rooted in God and the moral law. Why is it that the soldiers have a better spirit for war time than civilians? Because to them duty is primary; to civilians rights are primary.

Think of how many lawyers there are in the United States who are more interested in their fee than in the preservation of Justice; think of how many doctors there are who are more concerned about their livelihood than in someone else's life; think of how many teachers there are in the United States who teach because it pays well rather than because it is an opportunity to inculcate God's truth in the hearts of the young; think of how many capitalists there are who concentrate solely on their profits and their priorities rather than on the common good in war time; think of how many labor leaders and workers there are in the United States who are more interested in a closed shop, shorter hours, or their particular organization, or in higher wages than they are in serving those who earn one-twentieth as much by risking their lives for America!

But the soldiers, the sailors, the marines, the air corps — all these young men — most of whom earn but a dollar a day, never use the word "right"; they talk about a "job to do." It is not their salary that comes first; they sweat not for reward but for duty. And duty has a moral basis that makes brave men.

Let us of the civilian population imitate the soldiers and talk about duties. Such is the pattern of American life. In brief, if we want a victory over our enemies, let us first get on God's side and then go out and drive the devil out of them that they may be on God's side too!

PRAYER IN WAR TIME

This war is not a conflict of systems of poli1 tics, though a few superficial minds still think it is; it is a titanic struggle to decide whether the moral law of God shall be the basis of individual and social life, or the physical law of the ruthless sword.

The point to be emphasized is that since our conflict is with demonic forces, we can conquer them only by a national surrender to God and His Divine Son. This involves prayer, and prayer is never more necessary than in wartime.

Some of us pray but seldom, because we have kinks in our knees made by a pride that refuses to prostrate itself and acknowledge its dependence on God; others never pray because our ideas of religion are nothing but a jumble of Bible stories, mythologies, and sentiment.

If we believe only in a vague Power behind the universe, we will never pray, because we cannot pray to Power any more than we can pray to a stick of dynamite.

Neither can we pray if we confusedly believe in some "Great Architect" behind the universe, for the simple reason that he is behind the universe and not in it and with us.

But if that Power ever shared my weakness, and if that Wisdom ever shared my struggle, then I could pray. And that is Christ: the Power and the Wisdom of God is Love.

Where there is love, I can pray in spite of Power, for impatience can trust Love. Where there is love, I can pray in spite of Wisdom, for ignorance can trust Love. Only when we stand in the presence of Love do we become conscious of sin and the necessity of redeeming grace.

The young man in the Gospel could stand before the face of Incarnate Purity and say: "All these I have kept ever since I was a child" (Luke 18:21). But he failed in the test of Love.

Only when we stand before the self-denying heart of God on the Cross do we begin to realize not only our actual weakness, but our potential happiness. If you could persuade me that God could forgive me without all that the Cross means, you could persuade me that I could forgive myself — then I would never be wrong; then I would never need to pray.

In order to understand the meaning of prayer it may help to make three observations concerning its nature, two of which are negative.

First, the essence of prayer is not petition. The important word here is essence, because petition is a legitimate form of prayer.

We live in a conditional universe and many favors are granted on condition that we pray for them, as Our Lord said: "Ask, and you shall receive, that your joy may be full" (John 16:24). There are many favors hanging from the vault of heaven's blue on silken cords and prayer is the sword that cuts them.

What we are here emphasizing is that we must not pray on the constant assumption that the purpose of prayer is to get something, for if we identify getting with goodness, then when we do not get we may doubt the Goodness or the Power of God.

When our own will is denied we are too often like the little boy who wanted a gun for Christmas and called his father "bad," because he did not get it.

We meet that same spirit in those who say: "God let me down. I prayed that my brother wouldn't be sent to Hawaii, and he went last week."

These poor souls, if they really knew it, are identifying the Goodness of God with His readiness to do whatever they ask. They begin by praying to One Whom they admit knows more than they and has more power than they but they end by denying both.

They think of God as being reluctant to do good, which reluctance can be overcome only by petitions that sound like the pounding of fists of angry children, forgetful that God, not us, takes the initiative in giving. He loved us before He made us.

We do not know why God does not answer all our petitions, though He has told us that before we speak, He has already heard us.

St. James however suggests selfishness is one reason for unanswered prayer: "You covet and you do not have; you kill and envy, and cannot obtain. You quarrel and wrangle, and you do not have because you do not ask. You ask and do not receive, because you ask amiss, that you may spend it upon your passions" (James 4:2,3).

Many a man in the United States is living with only one eye or one finger, simply because his parents gave him exactly what he wanted on the Fourth of July.

I am sure that God has never answered and never will answer a baldheaded man's prayer for hair; and a woman could pray from now until the crack of doom, but God would never take the wart off the end of her nose.

Think these reflections through and you will understand why not all prayers are answered. God is omnipotent. He can do all things except one thing: He cannot please everybody.

And what a terrible world this would be if God answered the selfish prayers of everyone we think we could govern the world better than God.

Furthermore, when we pray we forget that in prayer God supplies our needs but not always our wants. Our Lord multiplied the loaves and fishes and gave to every man all that he needed.

Suppose however He multiplied gold bricks. How many among us would have been satisfied? Gold is a want; bread is a need.

Our Divine Lord on another occasion said that: "in praying, do not multiply words, as the

Gentiles do; for they think that by saying a great deal, they will be heard. So do not be like them; for your Father knows what you need before you ask him" (Matt. 6:7).

He knows our needs before we ask and has already arranged to supply them. The problem is, then: Do I want what He knows I need?

Suppose Our Dear Lord did come to us as we prayed for something and said: "I will give you anything you want. Choose it!" Would we not rather abandon our will and, counting on His Infinite Goodness, ask Him to do the choosing?

At Christmas when someone asks us what we want, do we not say, "You choose," knowing full well that his generosity will be greater than our daring?

Why not begin prayer that way, trusting in Him because He knows what is best. That is why petition is not the essence of prayer: Trust, for one thing, underlies it.

St. Paul three times prayed to be relieved of an affliction which was hindering his missionary work, but God did not answer the prayer.

Secondly, prayer is not an insurance policy, a bomb — proof shelter, a bullet-proof vest, a germicide. This observation is for those who think that God should suspend the operation of His natural laws every time they get into trouble.

Did He on Calvary suspend the law that a nail hit on the head by a hammer would pierce His blessed Hand?

The very ones who in time of peace think the business of God is to insure prosperity are the very ones who, in time of adversity, think the business of God is to grant immunity from harm.

Some prayers are nothing else but selfish expressions of the self-preservation instinct. Did not Our Lord say the sun shines on the just and the wicked? Therefore, may we not expect the bombs to fall on the wicked and the just?

If this world were all, if man had not an immortal soul, if the scales of justice were not balanced beyond the grave, if the loss of physical life were a greater evil than sin, then the Goodness of God could be identified with our good health, our fat bank deposits, and our freedom from wounds.

But since this world is the proving-ground of character, it must never be assumed that catastrophe is a special sign of sin. Our Divine Savior never spoke of perishing in the physical, but in the spiritual, sense.

When the Pharisee asked: "Rabbi, who has sinned, this man or his parents, that he should be born blind?" He answered, "Neither this man sinned, nor his parents, but the works of God were to be made manifest in him" (John 9:2-3).

It seems that some Galileans had broken a Roman law. Pilate heard of it and sent out soldiers to punish them. They arrived at the very moment the Galileans were worshipping, slew them then and there, and mingled their blood with their sacrifice.

Now it was likely the Judeans told him this story, for the Judeans hated the Galileans. And Our Lord answered and said: "Do you think that these Galileans were worse sinners than all the other Galileans because they suffered such things? I tell you, no; but unless you repent, you will all perish in the same manner" (Luke 13:2,3).

Our Lord then made reference to another tragedy, when a tower of Siloam fell and killed eighteen people. He asked again: "Do you think that they were more guilty than all the other dwellers in Jerusalem? I tell you, no; but unless you repent you shall all likewise perish in the same manner" (Luke 13:4,5).

Disaster does not disprove the goodness of God. A man can perish even though no tower fall on him, or a Pilate never slay him. He can die in bed surrounded by friends and flowers, with even soft music pouring into his ears; but he will be damned unless he repents of his sins.

What we seem to forget is that death is not the greatest evil; sin is. Hence "Do not be afraid of those who kill the body, but cannot kill the soul. But rather be afraid of him who is able to destroy both soul and body into hell" (Matt. 10:28).

The best lives are not always saved in battle; otherwise the heroes who die in battle and whose names we inscribed on our war memorials would all be wicked men. A St. Francis Assisi in a front line trench would have no guarantee that God would deflect a bullet to protect him.

But this much we could be sure of: no matter what would happen, nothing could turn him away from God, for as St. Paul says: "Now we know that for those who love God all things work together unto good, for those who, according to his purpose, are saints through his call" (Rom. 8:28).

Please do not misunderstand. It is right and just that we should pray for the safety of our loved ones; but we must not think of prayer always in terms of the suspension of God's natural law, or as a kind of safety device.

A chaplain in the last war said he heard some men praying when he wished they had gone over the top without it, for their prayer was but the mark of a broken will, a selfish desire, and a fear of death, a whimpering of formulas for personal protection in time of crisis.

The man alongside of him who, still unbroken and unbeaten, bore his gun like the Savior bore a scourge against thieves, put the whimpering man to shame.

A prayer for personal safety in time of great crisis when moral issues are at stake, is not what a man ought to be thinking about; it entails putting a greater value on physical life than on duty and justice.

The martyrs of old who were stretched on racks, tortured, and burned, were all men and women of prayer. They prayed for deliverance, like their Savior in the Garden; but they would not take it at the cost of faith or the denial of the Christ whom they bore in their souls. That was too high a price for saving their skins; so they lost their skins and saved their souls.

The answer to prayer, then, is not the escape from death, but the power to face it with trust in God.

This brings us to the third point: What prayer really is: the lifting up of our hearts and minds to God. More simply still, it is communion with God.

Prayer is like tuning in on a radio: It is a means of giving God access to our souls. In order to tune in a radio program you must set your dial to the proper wavelength. In like manner, in order to tune in to God, you must make your will correspond to His Divine Will.

Once this is done, just as you listen to the radio program to which you are attuned, so now you become obedient to the Divine Will to which your soul is attuned. Once the wavelength of our will is adjusted to the wavelength of God's will, we get what we want.

Then all prayers are answered; the program is just what we wanted. As St. John puts it: "And we know that he heareth us whatsoever we ask; we know that we have the petitions which we request of him" (John 5:15).

Prayer, then, is not so much asking God to do our will as asking God to do His will; its purpose is not so much to change God's will as it is to change our will.

We do not go to God with a blue-print of our own desires and ask God to rubber stamp it. Rather, we ask God to give us His blueprint and then we mobilize all our energies with His grace to fulfill it. Instead of Him approving our plans, we approve His.

Instead of going to God saying: "This is what I am going to do. Be with me, O Lord," we approach Him as St. Paul did at the moment of his conversion, and say: "'What shall I do, Lord' And the Lord said to me, 'Get up and go into Damascus, and there thou shalt be told of all that thou art destined to do" (Acts 22:10).

In wartime the proper approach is to ask God to use our collective wills and our national arms for His Holy Purposes, rather than to ask Him to serve our purposes. In prayer we do not ask God to fight on our side; we pray to fight on His side.

We pray not as Americans who happen to be Christians, but as Christians who happen to be Americans. We ask God not to do something for us, but to do something in us, that He may do something through us for the betterment of the world and the restoration of the moral order.

The essence of prayer therefore is a longing at all costs to be caught up in God's purposes.

A little child prayed for a thousand dolls for Christmas. She did not receive them. Her unbelieving father who had taunted both her and her mother for praying, one day cynically asked: "Well, God did not answer your prayers, did He?" To which the child gave the glorious answer: "O yes, He did! He said No!"

That was the child's way of putting what her Savior expressed in the Garden centuries ago. He prayed that the chalice of suffering might pass — "if it be possible." It was possible! His Father could have done it; twelve legions of angels, He said, could have routed His foes. But it would have been at the cost of not redeeming man.

The Divine purpose mattered more than His personal safety. God said, No! His prayer was answered: "Not my will but thine be done."

And is not that the way we pray every time we say the Our Father — "Thy will be done on earth as it is in heaven." Do we mean it?

Does it not imply a continual conversion and purgation of selfish, evil desires, that we may be caught up as an instrument to serve God's purposes and that peace, grounded on His justice, may reign throughout the world?

There is the answer to those who ask: "The Germans pray to God, the English pray to God, the Italians pray to God, the Americans pray to God. On whose side is God?"

Those who ask that question have not the vaguest idea of the meaning of prayer. They assume that God takes sides on the basis of geography, rather than on the basis of goodness. The answer is, that God is on the side of those who do His Will.

If we are with God, no man can be against us. Hence, if the German, the Englishman, the Italian, the American, all prayed as they should, they would all be praying for the same intention: "Thy will be done on earth as it is in heaven."

Then would be perfect unity on both sides of the battle front. Then we would have peace.

"Peace on earth to men of good will" — and short of that there will be no peace.

Pray then, unceasingly, that you may attain in this life, as much as the present condition will allow, a harmony with that Perfect Life, Truth, and Love which will constitute the blessedness of heaven. The more intensely we pray, the fewer will be our words.

In God there is but one word. The more we mean anything, the less expression we can find: "Would that I could utter the thoughts that are within me." Once this Divine love animates our life, then our conduct will be good. Prayer does not so much help our conduct as our conduct tests our prayers. If we think right, we will live right.

The greatest stupidity ever uttered was "It makes no difference what you believe, but only how you act." Nonsense! We act on our beliefs; if they are wrong, we live wrong. Prayer then comes before conduct.

Live with the God of love, in prayer, and you will act lovingly towards your neighbor. Think with the Christ on His Cross, and you will be charitable to your neighbor.

Your actions tell whether you ever pray not your ears. Prayer is not getting something; it is becoming something.

When we become good and glorify His name, then, we will get not only what we need, but what we want. We have His word for it: "Amen, amen, I say to you, if you ask the Father anything in my name, he will give it to you" (John 16:23).

Pray then that we may be victorious by being on God's side. Begin a monologue with God and it will end with a dialogue between you and the God Who redeems you.

Bring your sickness to the Divine Light, your wickedness to the sweet ointment of His Redemptive Cross, your hungry souls to His Communion rail, your imperfect sacrifices to His immolation on our altars. Pray for one reason — to bring yourselves in communion with a Purpose, God's Purpose, God's Will.

That's what most of us lack in our lives, a goal, a destiny, a loyalty beyond all fleeting enthusiasms.

If we are unhappy it is because our purpose is at odds with God's purpose which is best for us; we are criss-cross because we ignore the value of the Cross.

You carry a watch, but do not make your own time; you take it from the sky. You make your own journeys, but you do not draw your own map; you take it from Creation. In like manner, you live your own life, but you do not make your ultimate goal or perfection. You take it from God. Therefore Pray.

THE CRUCIFIXION

Looking out on the Four Horsemen spreading death, disease, war, and famine over the earth, we are tempted to ask: "Why does God let this happen?"

That is an incomplete sentence from the theological point of view. Finish it and it reads this way: "Why does God let this happen to Himself?

What a different light this casts on the tragedy of war to realize that in some mysterious way Christ is living, suffering, thirsting, starving, and being imprisoned and dying in us, and that this War is His Passion.

This does not mean that the historical Christ, Who was born of Mary, suffered under Pontius Pilate, and is now glorified at the right hand of the Father, suffers again in that same human nature; for having died once He can never die again.

But it does mean that the Christ Who is the Head of the Body which is the Church, does suffer again.

Just as Our Divine Lord took a human nature from the womb of Mary overshadowed by the Holy Spirit, so on the day of Pentecost He took from the womb of humanity a corporate nature, or a Church overshadowed by the same Pentecostal Spirit.

Through that Church He still continues to teach, to govern, and to sanctify.

That is why the Church is infallible, because Christ the Teacher teaches through it; that is why its authority is divine, because He the King governs through it; that is why the Sacraments are divine because He the Priest sanctifies through it.

This union of the Head and the Body is what St. Augustine calls the Totus Christus, the Whole Christ, the Church which is the prolongation through space and time of the Incarnation.

The union of Christ and the Church is as intimate, as the vine and the branches which have but one common life: "As the branch cannot bear fruit of itself unless it remain on the vine, so neither can you unless you abide in me" (John 15-4).

In the analogy of St. Paul, the unity of Christ with us, and we with one another, is like the unity of hand and foot, head and body, all with all.

If someone steps on your foot your head complains. St. Paul found out that this applies to the Mystical Body as well, when he was persecuting the Church of Damascus. The heavens opened and the glorified Christ said: "Saul, Saul, why dost thou persecute me?" (Acts 9-4).

In striking the Church which was His Body, Paul was striking Christ; "I am Jesus whom thou persecuteth."

And did not Our Lord Himself say that anyone who would do anything to one incorporated to Him would be doing it to Him, for example: "And whoever receives one such little child for my sake, receives me" (Matt. 18-5).

Did He not picture Himself as going through the world hungry, thirsty, imprisoned, and sick, and tell us that in serving them in His name we were serving Him: "Come, blessed of my Father, take possession of the kingdom prepared for you from the foundation of the world; for I was hungry and you gave me to eat; I was thirsty and you gave me to drink; I was a stranger and you took me in; naked and you covered me; sick and you visited me; I was in prison and you came to me" (Matt. 25-34-37).

Apply this now to the world war. Christ's life in His individual human nature is glorified; Christ's life in His Church and all incorporated to Him by baptism is not yet glorified. He is growing to His full stature in us as He grew to His full stature in the nature He took from Mary.

The crucifixion on Good Friday is not only something that happened 1900 years ago, it is something that is happening now as the Cross is erected in our midst today.

From a spiritual point of view there are no national causes; there is only the conflict of those who crucify Christ and those who are crucified with Him. Consider first how Christ is made to suffer today by those who crucify: Pilate and the executioners.

Judas still roams the world in the person of all those who were baptised to Christ and called to be one with Him, but who have fallen away from their high destiny by "selling out."

In the catalogue of Fascism, Nazism, and Communism you will find those who in their youth were signed with the sign of the Cross, sealed with the seal of salvation, and then like

Judas bargained away their Christian heritage for thirty pieces of silver from the coffers of a transitory political power.

Thumb over the lists of other nations and you will discover that those leaders who either welcomed international congresses of militant atheists to their midst, or turned their backs on the rights of religion, were those who, like Judas, were once called to be defenders of those rights and soldiers of Christ.

Those who do most harm to the cause of Christ are not those whose souls were left barren in their naturalism, but those called like Judas to live and move with the Son of God.

The Christ in the Garden of Gethsemane still has His lips blistered by a kiss, and, in His last gracious love to win them back, He still whispers: "Judas, dost thou betray the Son of Man with a kiss?" (Luke 22-38).

Pilate too still lives. He lives in all those teachers and jurists who deny an absolute; who feel that right and wrong are only points of view; who flatter themselves on their broadmindedness as they allow the mob to choose between Barabbas and Christ; who have a feeling that possibly Christ is the Son of God, but who would not assert it lest they lose favor with Caesar; who, when they are brought face to face unequivocally with Divine Truth, ask the same question asked by Pilate: "What is Truth" and then turn their back on it. Put the Creed therefore in the present tense: "Christ is suffering under Pontius Pilate."

The executioners still walk the earth: brutal, blind forces, which ignore the Divine, take orders from higher-ups, persecute the Christ in His Church and His Apostles, profane His Eucharistic Presence, nail His Mystical Body to a tree and then, with the calmness of their ancestors beneath Calvary, shake dice, "sit and watch," while before them is being re-enacted the tremendous drama of the world.

If there are those who crucify, there are those who are crucified with Christ — those who are hunted because they believe in Him and of whom Our Lord foretold: "If the world hates you, know that it has hated me before you" (John 15-18). "Yes, the hour is coming for everyone who kills you to think that he is offering worship to God" (John 16-2).

As Our Lord suffered on His Cross He looked forward to all times and all people and offered not only Himself but all the Members of His Body, the Church, to His Heavenly Father.

That oblation we actualize and complete in ourselves; in the language of St. Paul we say "What is lacking of the sufferings of Christ I fill up in my flesh for his body, which is the Church" (Col. 1-24).

How can we "fill up" the suffering of Christ? Was His Passion incomplete? Most certainly not.

It means that all our sufferings, pains and Calvary's were in His thoughts on the Cross and were offered to God the Father for us, but they were wanting" in the sense that they had not yet been endured in "our flesh."

That the Passion be completed in any soul is necessary that the part assigned to Him be realized and actualized and suffered in his body. Each of us therefore must finish in his life and in his soul the vision of the dying Christ.

The precise manner in which we concur in the Passion of Christ and give value to our sufferings and communicate with Calvary is, for Catholics, the Holy Sacrifice of the Mass. Because we are in Christ, we are given a chance to cooperate with Him, as we do in the creation. God has called us to share His causality and His freedom.

Man needs a habitation. God, instead of building it Himself, gave man the power to build it with the materials from His bountiful hand.

Man needs food; God does not serve the table — He calls man to share His creative power by sowing the seed and tilling the fields.

And so with Redemption. The Son of God has given us the sublime vocation of sharing in the "fellowship of the Cross"; He has called each of us to be a redeemer with a small "I" as He is the Redeemer with a capital "R". To each of us He says: Here is a splinter from the Cross that I have been carrying from the foundation of the world.

It is this consciousness of sharing in Christ's redemption that gives to some men patience and joy in suffering, for in Christ they see that their sacrifices can be taken up into His eternal sacrifice, and can be made creative and redemptive.

We are not to think of God as standing outside the sufferings of the world, apart and aloof, in the untroubled serenity of heaven. God is not a spectator to the drama of suffering; He has come down as its greatest Tragediau and as sin's greatest Victim.

If He points to a forest and bids us enter, it is because His feet have already made the pathway through the thickets and the thorns; if He bids us take up a Cross daily and follow Him, it is because He has already borne the brunt of it on His shoulders.

God is not outside the tears and the tragedy of life; in every pang that rends the heart of a man, woman, or child, God has His share.

We cannot meet a cross in our respective walks of life but that He already took it at the foot of Pilate's temple and made it the badge of His glory and the symbol of a Christian.

We cannot have feet tired and worn from the service of others but that His own were calloused from going about doing good and nailed to a Cross for having been too good.

We cannot have the sorrow of losing friends or a mother but that He Himself already felt the rent in His Own Heart, as He left a friend to a mother on the gibbet of a Cross.

If then He is in us, we shall overcome the world as He did, by the same love.

Our Divine Lord had more enemies than any man who ever lived, and perhaps He had fewer friends, if we are to judge from those who stood by Him in His Passion.

His enemies were our enemies too, for they were the enemies of all that is Christian for all times; and yet when He died He made them His friends through the power of His love and His Friendship and His surrender to death.

"Greater love than this no man hath, that He lay down His life for His friends."

As He looked out on the world from that Cross and saw all His enemies who had brought evil into the world, not only for His time but unto the consummation of the world, He saw them not as people to be hated and despised, but as wounded and twisted and mutilated souls not able to heal themselves.

His Divine Love poured out upon them, for the Son of man came not to destroy sinners but to save them.

If, then, Christ is suffering in us, we have the responsibility of loving those who make us suffer, that we, like Him, may redeem them. Then, if our lot in war is the lot of tragedy and suffering and sacrifice, it will be done gladly because He is in us once more, redeeming a world.

It was this vision that sustained the soldier as he carried his pack, and the true Christian soldier, like Joyce Kilmer, will think of his task in the light of the Passion of Christ:

"My shoulders ache beneath my pack,
  (Lie easier, Cross, upon His back.)

"I march with feet that burn and smart,
(Tread, Holy Feet, upon my heart.)

"Men shout at me who may not speak,
(They scourged Thy back and smote Thy cheek.)

 "I may not lift a hand to clear
My eyes of salty drops that sear.

" (Then shall my fickel soul forget
Thy Agony of Bloody Sweat?)

"My rifle hand is stiff and numb,
(From Thy pierced palm red rivers come.)
"Lord, Thou didst suffer more for me
Than all the hosts of land and sea.

"So let me render back again
This millionth of Thy gift! Amen."

(Prayer of a Soldier in France, by Joyce Kilmer)

Because we are in Christ, we will try to reproduce the sentiments of Christ and His Cross:

To those who make us suffer, who nail us to a Cross, we will say: "Father, forgive them, for they do not know what they do."

They thought, O Heavenly Father, they were crucifying a man; and they think now they are crucifying a human institution, when in reality they are, like Paul before his conversion, persecuting You.

They do not know their every nail is aimed at Thee, O Christ. They do not know what Peace you bring. "Father, forgive them, for they do not know what they do" (Luke 23:34).

Two thieves did blaspheme Thee on the Cross, and yet one of them was saved.

Many too are suffering in the world today without solving its mystery in Thee, cursing and blaspheming Thee from their beds and their battlefields.

Give us Thy vision, O Jesus, that we may never despair of converting even those who blaspheme Thee. Grant that some of them, like the thief on the right, may hear Thy

Words: "Amen I say to thee, this day thou shalt be with me in paradise" (Luke 23-43).

From Thy Cross, Christ, Thou didst command Thy dear Mother to Thy beloved disciple, and Thy beloved disciple to Thy dear Mother. May we, nailed on our cross like Thee, see that when duty fastens us that we stay to do Thy Will and if need be, make the surrender of loved ones and family. "Woman, behold thy son ... Behold thy mother" (John 19:27).

When darkness did so envelop Thy Cross, and the sun hid its light at high noon; when suspended between Heaven and earth, Thou didst feel that both earth and heaven had rejected Thee — Thou didst never once lose in Thy human nature Thy hold on God, crying: "My God, my God, why hast thou forsaken me?" (Matt. 27-46).

Give us strength, O Jesus, when we seem abandoned, in darkness and in pain, when all seems lost, and when Heaven never answers our "whys," still to cry out in undying force, "My God, my God."

When Thou didst turn to me and say, "I thirst" (John 19:28), Thou meant not a thirst for water but a thirst for love from the hearts Thou hadst made.

123

May the chalice of Thy Gethsemane, filled with the wine of suffering, be unto my lips as salt; may it make me thirst to spread Thy Name and love before men, so that in the end I may measure my life not by the wine I drank but by the wine I poured forth.

Under Thy Cross men challenged, "If he is the King of Israel, let him now come down from the cross, and we will believe him" (Matt. 27-42). But Thou didst stay until the task was done and in triumph did cry out: "It is consummated!" (John 19-30).

O Jesus, grant that, whatever may be my lot in life, whether it be in light or darkness, You will empower me to hold to my faith, to fight the good fight, to run the course, to stay on the Cross until the evening comes so that I can say in triumph too: "It is consummated!"

Thou didst give Thy Body and Blood to earth, Thou wilt soon give Thy Body to the tomb, Thy Mother to John, and John to Thy mother; but Thy Spirit Thou didst keep for the Father.

Grant that I may keep my spirit too amidst the wars and sorrows of this world so that at the end I can give it back to Thee from whence it came.

Let the last word of my life be: "Father, into thy hands I commend my spirit" (Luke 23:46).

THE DIVINE PATH TO VICTORY

Celebrating Easter in a world that is more like Good Friday, and hearing the chants of Peace amidst the explosions of war, makes us wonder what lesson this Blessed Feast can offer in these tragic days.

The answer is to be found in two scenes in the life of Our Blessed Lord, that reveal the Divine Path to Victory.

The first scene takes place in the Carden of Gethsemane when the Savior, in the full majesty of His Person, goes out to meet the devil in the guise of Judas, and the soldiers who came with swords and clubs to apprehend Him.

Reminding them that no one taketh His life away, but He lays it down of Himself, He now surrenders Himself into their hands with these words: "This is your hour and the power of darkness.

The important word here is hour, for apparently Evil has its hour and uses it to turn out the lights of the world and deliver it over to the Stygian darkness of despair.

The second scene took place earlier in His Public Life when the Pharisees sought to get rid of Him by making Him fearful of Herod, whom they said intended to kill Him.

'The supreme value of the story is in the answer He gave. In effect He said: "Go and say to that fox, 'Behold, I cast out devils and perform cures today and tomorrow, and the third day I am to end my course.

Nevertheless, I must go my way today and tomorrow and the next day, for it cannot be that a prophet perish outside Jerusalem'" (Luke 13:32, 33).

In other words, go tell that fox who has a mind to kill me, that he is helpless; he cannot kill me until I have done my work, and I have three days' work to do.

This was figurative language: Two of these days are for works of wonder convincing men of His Divinity, but the third day will be the day of mystery and perfection. The important word here is day.

Setting the two scenes together there emerges this lesson: Evil has its hour, but God has His day. And that evil hour is part of God's day, inseparable from it, one with it.

Unless the seed has its "hour" when it falls to the ground and dies, it will never have its "day" when it springs forth into life.

Without that hour of war with evil, there would never be this day of Peace; without the Cross there would never be the empty tomb; without Good Friday, there would never be an Easter Sunday; without the crown of thorns there would never be the halo of light.

And there is the answer to our Easter query: "How can we celebrate Easter in a world that is a Good Friday?" By seeing in this war the operation of God's law, that without this hour of suffering and sacrifice we might never come to a day of peace and resurrection of our national life.

Peace is not a passive but an active condition; it is not something given, but something achieved. Our Lord never said, Blessed are the peaceful, but blessed are the peace makers.

Peace must be made, won in battle, as He won it. Good Friday was not a day of appeasement; therefore Easter will not be a day of false peace — God hates peace in those who are destined for war! Evil has its hour but God has His day.

It is highly significant that on the day of triumph He was recognized through some gesture connected with that hour; in no single instance did they perceive His glory except by looking through the windows of Calvary:

Mary Magdalen came to the knowledge of His Glory through the sepulchre where they laid Him in the hour of defeat.

Peter and John perceived the day of triumph through the winding sheets in which He was wrapped in the hour of His ignominious death.

The disciples on the way to Emmaus recognized the Conqueror in the newness of His day, at the breaking of Bread — which recalled the deliverance of His Body in the hour of darkness.

Thomas, the doubter, saw His Divinity through fingers put in hands and hands thrust inside — the relics of an hour's battle with the power of evil in which the slain had the victory.

So much is the "hour" the part of His "day" that in the triumph of His resurrection — day

He keeps the scars received in the hour of defeat.

And He keeps them for all eternity; even on the last day when He will come in glory to judge the living and the dead, He will bear them as pledges of His victory. He is Prince of Peace because He was Captain of wars and Lord of hosts.

Soldiers wear medals for bravery but He keeps the scars of the hour in which He fought for peace. The Via Crucis is the Via Pacis. The way of the Cross is the way of Peace.

To pass through the hour of evil is in itself no guarantee of a day of peace — we must pass through it with faith in His Resurrection.

"The thief on the left passed through evil but it profited him nothing, for his sufferings were not borne in Christ. The thief on the right, on the contrary, passed through his hour in union with Christ, and therefore came to His Day: "This Day ... Paradise."

As St. Paul says: "This saying is true: if we have died with him, we shall also live with him" (2 Tim. 2:11); but our death must be in Him.

Apply this lesson that only those who pass through Calvary's hour with Him shall ever come to the Day of Victory.

Look out upon Holland, Belgium, France, Germany, Finland, Italy, the Philippines, Greece, Russia, the Balkan States, Mexico, Spain! I speak not of those who suffer, but of those who do so in union with Him.

Like the Christ, these souls are having their hour — the hour of darkness, of famine, of persecution.

Above all the battle flags of the world, beyond the din of national slogans, the scheming of foxes, the debates of politics, and the selfish clashes of economic forces — there is one common bond uniting them all who are in Christ.

They have all been kissed by some Judas, smitten by some soldier, misjudged by some Caiphas, mocked by some Herod, and crucified under some Pilate, in this their hour of darkness; but if the Easter law hold true — and it does — to the extent their sufferings are one with His, there is the guarantee of their resurrection.

Not because of any new shuffling of politicians or any new theory in economics,

will they come to greatness, for politics again
will fail, economists again will blunder, foxes
will be caught in their own traps; but because
they have been signed with the sign of the
Cross, sealed with the seal of salvation —
because they have borne the Cross in Christ
— they will rise with Christ!

This war is the sowing of the seed. Evil has
its hour, but God will have His Day.

Apply the lesson now to our own country. If
it be true that those who have already had
their "hour" with Christ will have their "day"
with Him, then the inverse is true: We shall
have our day of victory only on condition that
we have our hour of darkness with Christ.

We want Victory with Justice in this war.
But Easter teaches us that there can be no
true Day of Victory unless we pass through
the Hour of struggle against evil in union with
the Savior. As Our Risen Lord told His
Disciples on the road to Emmaus, "Know you
not that the Son of man must suffer in order
to enter into His Glory."

We have already begun to pass through
that Hour of sacrifice, not so much because of
our own choice, but because our enemies have
forced us into it. Like the Savior on Calvary we
are already being stripped, not of our

garments, as He was, but of our rags of "self-righteousness."

First of all, we are beginning to die to that false notion that there is no evil. Up to a few years ago, we denied there was a devil. Now we are pointing our fingers across the waters saying: "They are wrong; they are devils."

But how can they be wrong, unless there is a right; and how can there be a devil unless there is a God? Our enemies have thus driven us into an Hour where we re-discovered God.

We are also being stripped of the false rags of "self-expression." Until a few years ago most all our educators denied the necessity of discipline and restraint. Now we are dying to that false concept and like Nicodemus beginning to see that unless nations, like men, are reborn they cannot enter into glory.

Finally, we are being stripped of the rags of Progress. Up to this time, we believed that Progress is in an ever-mounting straight line, or in a spiral ever-ascending; that we became better by the mere fact that we live; that blind cosmic forces of evolution were pushing us on to become supermen.

This war reveals to us just the contrary, viz. that no life becomes better unless it dies to its lower self.

This spring is not an ascending progress from last spring, but through the death of an old spring. So must all nations and civilizations die in their hour of darkness, before they may come to the day of their victory.

There will be an hour of humiliation — of that there is no doubt. Our choice as a nation is not between being humbled and not being humbled; it is rather, Who shall humble us, our enemies or ourselves.

Would we, as a defeated nation, be more moral and just and Christian than we would be as a victorious, revengeful nation? If the only way that we could be bettered would be by defeat, then we may expect it.

But it is not the only way. Instead of being humbled by enemies, we can humiliate ourselves by recognizing that only by and through God and His Redemption can we come to victory.

We have not yet entered into the fullness of that idea, but only the beginning of it. We have yet to complete the lesson and to learn that man of and by himself cannot defeat the devil.

We already know the power of our enemy; we have not yet learned our hidden strength that in Christ we can do all things. "Without me you can do nothing!"

Our choice is like that which Joshua presented to his people when he said to them: "Choose this day which pleases you; whom you would rather serve, whether the gods your fathers served in Mesopotamia or the Lord your God."

Our answer must be as that of Joshua. "But as for me and my house we will serve the Lord."

If an hour comes in our national life when labor will lift up its hands, as Christ lifted His in the carpenter shop, in service to the Father; if capital, like Joseph of Arimathea, will give of its possessions for the service of Christ; if women, like Magdalen, will bring their spices to anoint Him; if educators, like Nicodemus, will come in the dark to find the truth which is His; if the soldiers, like the one at the foot of the Cross, share the wine of their life with Him; if we all begin to see Him wounded in the wounded, hidden in the lost, destitute in the destitute, if we all enter this work of sacrifice as He entered the garden, then we need never fear the outcome — we have already won, only the news has not yet leaked out. We shall have our day of victory in Him, because we have already had our hour of darkness.

If there is any figure that adequately describes this lesson, it is that of the eagle. Eagles generally build their nests high in the mountains and most often over great crevices, canyons, and precipices.

When finally the young are hatched, the mother eagle, in virtue of an instinct implanted in her by Almighty God, begins to stir up the nest and scatter the twigs that cradled the infancy of its young. It nudges one of the eaglets to the edge of the nest, where, catching the vision of the yawning depth below, it shrinks back again into the safety of its nest.

But the mother bird, through the infallible urge of its Creator, finally succeeds in pushing the young over the edge of the nest.

Down and down it falls, its feeble wings fluttering in vain to bear it up against what must seem to it catastrophe and death on the rocks below.

But just before the eaglet crashes in the fearful depths, the mother bird swoops under it, catches it in her great wings, bears it aloft into the sky, and then, debarking its living cargo, allows the young one to flutter again and fall—but not to death.

Again the mother bird saves her young from catastrophe, lifts it again unto the sky, and repeats the process until the eaglet at last has learned to fly.

Moses must have seen some such scene as that for he makes use of it to explain God's dealing with the nations. As the eagle stirs the nest of her young, so does God stir up the nations!

Is not the war just like that, if we could but see it aright? Have we not been as the little eaglet, quite satisfied with the little nest we made in the world; were we not so smug, self-satisfied, and complacent that we forgot we had immortal souls, forgot that these souls have wings and were destined by God to carry us to higher realms beyond the earth?

So God, like an eagle, had to stir up our national nests, toss us out of our smug earthliness, let us fall near to disaster before we realized we had need of Him for salvation.

For unless we had that hour of darkness we could never have the day of light; for evil has its hour but God will have His day.

And that is indeed an apt figure of America, for our symbol is not the lion going about seeking whom it may devour, not the fox that would sneak up on its prey to destroy, not the vulture that waits for life to become carrion, but, in the full consciousness of what God destined us to be, our Country chose as its symbol the eagle flying upward and upward, unto the sky beyond the "troubled gateways of the stars," across the "margent of the world," up beyond the hid battlements of eternity, up beyond the hour of darkness to the Day of Everlasting Victory in Christ Jesus Our Lord!

ACKNOWLEDGMENTS

I want to thank Almighty God for the health of mind, body, and spirit to put together these reflections.

To my good wife, Isabel, my children, and my grandchildren, who keep me young at heart and are truly a blessing from God. Thank you for sharing in my joy.

I wish to express my gratitude to members of the Archbishop Fulton John Sheen Foundation in Peoria, Illinois — in particular, to the Most Rev. Daniel R. Jenky, C.S.C., Bishop of Peoria, for your leadership and fidelity to the cause of Sheen's canonization and the creation of this book.

To Julie Enzenberger, O.C.V., who repeated to me time and time again Sheen's words: "Believe the incredible, and you can do the impossible."

To the staff and volunteers at Sophia Institute Press for their invaluable assistance in helping to publish the writings of Archbishop Fulton J. Sheen. I am indebted to them for this great work.

To the many seminarians, priests, religious, bishops, and cardinals I have met during this journey. Always remember the words of Archbishop Sheen that "The priest is not his own."

To the tens of thousands of people I have met in my travels, giving presentations about Archbishop Fulton J. Sheen at parishes, conferences, universities, high schools, church groups, and even pubs: thank you for sharing with me your many "Sheen Stories." I truly cherish each one of them.

And lastly, to Archbishop Fulton J. Sheen, whose teachings on prayer, the sacraments, our Lord's Passion, and His Seven Last Words continue to inspire me to love God more and to appreciate the gift of the Church. His teachings and his encouragement to make a Holy Hour each day has been a true gift in my life. May I be so blessed as to imitate Archbishop Sheen's love for the saints, the sacraments, the Eucharist, and for the Mother of God. May the Good Lord grant him a very high place in Heaven!

— Al Smith

ABOUT THE AUTHOR

Fulton J. Sheen

(1895–1979)

Fulton John Sheen was born in El Paso, Illinois, in 1895. In high school, he won a three-year university scholarship, but he turned it down to pursue a vocation to the priesthood. He attended St. Viator College Seminary in Illinois and St. Paul Seminary in Minnesota. In 1919, he was ordained a priest for the Diocese of Peoria, Illinois. He earned a licentiate in sacred theology and a bachelor of canon law at the Catholic University of America and a doctorate at the Catholic University of Louvain, Belgium.

Sheen received numerous teaching offers but declined them in obedience to his bishop and became an assistant pastor in a rural parish. Having thus tested his obedience, the bishop later permitted him to teach at the Catholic University of America and at St. Edmund's College in Ware, England, where he met G. K. Chesterton, whose weekly BBC radio broadcast inspired Sheen's later NBC broadcast, The Catholic Hour (1930–1952).

In 1952, Sheen began appearing on ABC in his own series; Life Is Worth Living. Despite being given a time slot that forced him to compete with Milton Berle and Frank Sinatra, the dynamic Sheen enjoyed enormous success and in 1954 reach tens of millions of viewers, non-Catholics as well as Catholics.

When asked by Pope Pius XII how many converts he had made, Sheen responded, "Your Holiness, I have never counted them. I am always afraid if I did count them, I might think I made them, instead of the Lord."

Sheen gave annual Good Friday homilies at New York's St. Patrick's Cathedral, led numerous retreats for priests and religious, and preached at summer conferences in England.

"If you want people to stay as they are," he said, "tell them what they want to hear. If you want to improve them, tell them what they should know." This he did, not only in his preaching but also in the more than ninety books he wrote. His Peace of Soul was sixth on the New York Times best-seller list.

Sheen served as auxiliary bishop of New York (1951–1966) and as bishop of Rochester (1966–1969).

Two of his great loves were for the Blessed Mother and the Eucharist. He made a daily holy hour before the Blessed Sacrament, from which he drew strength and inspiration to preach the gospel and in the presence of which he prepared his homilies. "I beg [Christ] every day to keep me strong physically and alert mentally in order to preach His gospel and proclaim His Cross and Resurrection," he said. "I am so happy doing this that I sometimes feel that when I come to the good Lord in Heaven, I will take a few days' rest and then ask Him to allow me to come back again to this earth to do some more work."

Sheen also said that "the greatest love story of all time is contained in a tiny white host." This was the love that transformed him. His daily Eucharistic Holy Hour was legendary. From the day of his ordination to the day of his death, Sheen spent an hour a day praying in the presence of the Blessed Sacrament. From his office desk, through an open door, he could gaze upon the tabernacle at all times. His union with Christ enabled him to more fully, more accurately and more convincingly lead others to Christ in all he said and did. Sheen was a man of many talents and accomplishments, but it was Christ who enabled him to use them in the best ways.

The good Lord called Fulton Sheen home in 1979. His television broadcasts, now on tape, and his books continue his earthly work of winning souls for Christ. Sheen's cause for canonization was opened in 2002. In 2012, Pope Benedict XVI declared him "Venerable." In 2019, Pope Francis approved a miracle attributed to the intercession of the Venerable Fulton Sheen, clearing the way for his beatification.

Books Available Through Bishop Sheen Today Publishing

The Rainbow of Sorrow

The Seven Last Words

Calvary and the Mass

Love One Another

The Cross and the Beatitudes

The Cross and the Crisis

Love One Another

Victory Over Vice

The Seven Virtues

For God and Country

God and War

The Divine Verdict

God Love You

The Seven Last Words Explained

The Priest Is Not His Own

The Cross and the Crib

Philosophies at War

The Seven Last Words of Christ Explained

Father, Forgive Them for They Know Not What They Do.

This Day Thou Shall Be with Me in Paradise

Woman Behold Your Son; Behold Your Mother

My God! My God! Why Hast Thou Forsaken Me?

I Thirst

It is Finished

Father Into Your Hands I Commend My Spirit

Liberty, Equality and Fraternity

Missions and the World Crisis

Seven Words to the Cross

Seven Pillars of Peace

The Holy Hour Prayer Book

Seven Words of Jesus & Mary

www.bishopsheentoday.com